Painters and Peasants in the Nineteenth Century

Painters and Peasants in the Nineteenth Century

by

RICHARD R. BRETTELL

and

CAROLINE B. BRETTELL

SKIRA

© 1983 by Editions d'Art Albert Skira S.A., Geneva

All rights reserved. No part of this book may be
reproduced in any manner whatsoever without permission of
Editions d'Art Albert Skira S.A.
89 Route de Chêne, 1208 Geneva, Switzerland

Library of Congress Catalog Card Number: 83-9699

ISBN: 2-605-00027-3

Printed in Switzerland

CONTENTS

INTRODUCTION

Friedrich Nerly (1807-1878):
Italian Girl with Copper Pots, c. 1830.
Pencil and wash.

No study of the peasant in European art during the nineteenth century can meet all the demands of so large a subject. Peasants are represented in countless pictures, from Salon painting to popular illustrations, and described or commented on in every kind of writing, from great novels to travel journals. Thousands of books have been written about the European peasantry since it became a subject of interest in the eighteenth century, and reading the twentieth-century historical and anthropological literature on the French peasant alone would require a lifetime. To grasp the full significance of every peasant image, one would have to know all the major European languages as well as many dialects and regional *patois*. To make suitable generalizations about the function of the peasant image in modern society, one would have to know a good deal more than anyone does at present about the European picture market in the nineteenth century.

We have decided, however, to brave these perils and take on the subject at its broadest. In our looking and reading, we have omitted no category of picture or text and have preferred to range widely rather than probe deeply. It must be understood, of course, that our knowledge has certain centres and margins and that we, like too many students of modern culture, know more about France than about any other European country. We have tried to get away from this professional francophile tendency in our selection of pictures and, to a lesser extent, of texts. Yet it must be admitted that, in spite of our efforts, this account of the peasant in European art in the nineteenth century is rooted in France.

What is a peasant? The posing of this simple question raises a host of other questions which can never be resolved. There are, quite simply, many definitions of the peasantry. In some, peasants are rural peoples who live "outside time," who eat what they produce and gather, and who make what they live in and wear. Defined in this manner, peasants are essentially "primitive" peoples, the purity of whose lives is threatened by any attempt to enter them. It is fair to say that, using this extreme definition, there were almost no peasants in nineteenth-century Europe. The same problems are encountered when one attempts to define the peasantry in terms of the survival of their feudal ties, or as those rural workers who are subject to the aristocracy. Such definitions involve other, thornier matters. We have concluded, after reading a great deal of nineteenth-century literature, that the word peasant in many major European languages was used loosely throughout the century to mean rural labourers. Perhaps the best definition we can provide is one invented by John Gagliardo in his brilliant study of the changing image of the German peasant in the eighteenth and nineteenth centuries: those "who live in the country and practise agriculture themselves as their life's work."

Unfortunately, the breadth of the definition does little to help us cut down the sheer number of pictures to be discussed. We have therefore imposed certain limitations. Our account is generally illustrated with paintings, many of the more important of which were publicly exhibited at the time they were made and some of which were reproduced so often that they became "icons" or, perhaps better, "emblems" of the peasantry. We have included what are now called popular illustrations sparingly, mostly to give the reader a brief glimpse into another arena of the public image of the peasant. We have virtually omitted drawings and small-edition prints from discussion and have included only a sample of the many book illustrations in travel guides and novels. These decisions have been made to allow for a certain consistency in so sweeping a survey.

It is also worth remarking that we have not been swayed in our selection of paintings by modern notions of quality. Although many, indeed most, of the paintings illustrated are in museums throughout the world, perhaps less than a quarter would be considered by those museums to be of "masterpiece quality"; to play, that is, an important role in the total history of modern art. Our decision to include works by lesser artists has not been made because we want to elevate their status. We know that Millet was then and remains today a greater painter than Breton, and that Pissarro is more important than Bastien-Lepage. However, within the public context of the nineteenth century, paintings by Breton, Lhermitte, and Bastien-Lepage, to name only the more notable of the innumerable minor painters of rural life, were as responsible for the propagation of the image of the peasant as those of Millet or Pissarro. We have always remembered that we are writing about pictures of the peasant in the nineteenth century and not about masterpieces which represent peasants. Fortunately, the more important paintings often tell us a great deal more than lesser works about the meaning and beauty of the peasant image.

There are two general ways to organize a book about the peasant in European art in the nineteenth century and we have used both rather than one or the other. The first section of the book discusses the peasant image in terms of a roughly chronological history of style. We have defined three sequentially overlapping phases in the history of the peasant image and these are correlated, again roughly, with the types of peasants represented. If this section puts the peasant image into time, the second section attempts to define the broad outlines of a "functional" analysis of the peasant image, and it takes as its major assumption the notion that works of art embody and communicate certain norms or ideals, sometimes clearly and sometimes with difficulty. Most of these ideals tell us perhaps more about the society for whom the pictures are produced—in this case, the bourgeoisie—than they do about the peasants represented. The peasant image imposed ideals upon the peasant, many of which were undoubtedly present in peasant culture, but in different forms. We have learned that, as in all the mimetic arts, the describer cannot help imposing his own culture upon his representation of another one.

It is perhaps wise to remember, however, that nineteenth-century Europeans were often more familiar with rural life than we are today. Many city-dwellers and several "peasant painters" were of rural or peasant origin. Peasant families moved almost daily into the cities of Europe. It is also true that nineteenth-century travel was slower than that of the twentieth and that rural tourism was part of the life of every wealthy or educated townsman. Even today, the country or weekend house, no matter how small, is an integral part of European urban life to a much greater extent than it is in America. Looked at from the vantage-point of rural tourism and vacations, the peasant image is but one part of the exploitation of the country by the city which has been so well studied by Raymond Williams. Indeed, there are countless nineteenth-century texts which contrast the "natural" qualities of country life and country people with the artificiality of the city and which, in effect, urge urban readers to "improve themselves" (or their fellow inhabitants) by spending time in the country. In this way, the peasantry was less understood than "used" by city-dwellers and, no matter how flattering their view of country people, it was generally either incomplete or false.

As many modern writers about the peasantry have shown, the nineteenth-century peasant was as confused about the bewildering changes in modern culture as were his urban contemporaries. The peasant, in fact, inhabited a world almost as complex, as image conscious, and as nervous as the then modern townsman. Yet the important consideration in any understanding of the peasantry in the nineteenth century is that the peasant image triumphed over the peasant. The pervasive and essentially late-Romantic vision of the "folk" apart from industrial expansion and modern problems preoccupied Europeans of the nineteenth century. They actively imagined a peasantry which was timeless, politically naïve, and internally consistent. Perhaps with the single exception of the almost pagan peasants of Brittany represented in the paintings of Gauguin, Bernard, and Sérusier, the peasant image—whether anarchist, Napoleonic, Republican, nationalist, regionalist, avant-garde, academic, early, or late—was the artists' attempt at a unifying symbol for a confused, cautious, and changing Europe.

I

STYLE AND THE PEASANT IMAGE

THE CLASSICAL TRADITION:
The Northern Artist and the Italian Peasant, 1820-1900

In the beginning of the century, the man who did not wear a uniform was not a proper subject for art unless he lived in Italy as a peasant or a robber. That is to say, painters were either archaeologists or tourists; when they did not dive into the past, they sought their romantic ideal in distance... Only in Rome, in Naples, and in Tuscany was it thought possible to meet with human beings who had not become vulgar and hideous under the influence of civilization.

Richard Muther, The History of Modern Painting, 1907

In 1822 the young Swiss artist Léopold Robert painted a beautiful, anonymous peasant woman from central Italy against the background of her native landscape. There is nothing remarkable for the 1820s in the style of the painting, especially for a student of David and Girardet. Indeed, its neo-classicism is marked, from the hardened clarity of its contours to the balanced repose of its composition. Its sources are to be found in "high art," less that of classical antiquity than of the Italian High Renaissance. The composition refers back to Leonardo's *Mona Lisa*, and the style and palette to the young Raphael. There are perhaps less distant art historical connections between the *Girl of Procida* and Ingres' famous portrait of *Mlle Rivière* exhibited with those of her parents at the Salon of 1805. Yet what is remarkable, one is tempted to say radical, about Robert's painting is that such efforts were made to ennoble a common peasant woman. A peasant subject was not in itself unusual; thousands of prints and painted studies of the Italian peasantry pre-date Robert's painting. But a peasant imbued with the grandeur of High Renaissance painting was another matter altogether. Why did Robert paint such a picture? The reasons were most certainly complex and are not completely decipherable. Yet it is clear that such a picture could not have been painted very much earlier and that it was to become part of an artistic vanguard of peasant genre which is largely forgotten today.

Léopold Robert (1794-1835):
Girl of Procida, 1822.

Léopold Robert (1794-1835):
*Harvesters Arriving
in the Pontine Marshes*, 1830.

The search for subjects was a perennial and difficult one for artists young and old in the 1820s. The repertoire of classical themes was largely exhausted; there were hundreds, even thousands, of representations of the great scenes from classical history and mythology, and in the early years of the Restoration painters in France had begun already to turn to scenes of French and English Renaissance history for new motifs. Robert, however, was in Italy, and his search for subjects led him away from northern historical themes towards the beauty of the humble people of Italy whom he and others considered to be survivors of the ancient Romans. To Robert, and to many contemporary viewers of his paintings, the idealized peasant woman with her ethnographically exact cos-

tume and jewelry was as beautiful and noble as an ancient Roman matron, a Renaissance lady, or a young woman of the *haute bourgeoisie* in France. Indeed, she inhabited an almost "time-less" realm associated more with the seasonal rhythms of agricultural work than with a system of lineage, aesthetic and actual, which connected both the paintings and their subjects to classical antiquity. In a sense, these paintings denied contemporaneity to their humble subjects.

Like most decisions, Robert's choice to paint modern Italian peasants was not made in isolation. Rather, he was encouraged to explore these subjects by a French artist, Jean-Victor Schnetz, who had painted Italian peasants as early as the year of Robert's arrival in Italy, 1818,

Léopold Robert (1794-1835):
*Return from the Pilgrimage to the
Madonna dell'Arco*, 1827.

and who continued to specialize in peasant genre throughout the 1820s and 1830s. Both Schnetz and Robert, as well as their contemporaries Michallon and Haudebourt-Lescot, approached their subjects with all the training and techniques of the neo-classical artist, and the images they created were to be important additions to the Paris Salons until the death of Robert in 1835. It was surely for these Salons, as well as the informed art market around them, that the peasant paintings of Schnetz and Robert were meant, and it was precisely their subject that made their pictures stand out from the history paintings, historical landscapes, portraits, and still lifes which separated their efforts from those of the genre painters of French life like Boilly. Robert himself, in a letter to his friend Brandt written in October 1822, put the matter succinctly: "I was lucky, I must admit. I deliberately chose an unfamiliar genre, and people happened to like it. It is always an advantage to come first. When I went to Italy, I was struck by these Italian figures, by their remarkable customs and ways, their picturesque and uncouth clothing. I set out to render this as truthfully as possible, but above all with the simplicity and nobility which one cannot help noticing in the Italian people and which is a trait inherited from their ancestors."

Robert and Schnetz painted both individual peasants and carefully composed peasant groupings with enormous zeal in the 1820s. By 1827 Robert had finished his first masterpiece, the *Return from the Pilgrimage to the Madonna*

15

dell'Arco, a painting which he conceived as the first of a series of four canvases devoted to three intertwined themes: first, characteristic scenes of humble life in Italy; second, the four major places in Italy—the countryside around Naples, the Roman Campagna, Tuscany, and Venice; and, lastly, the four seasons. The fête of the Madonna dell'Arco was a pentecostal festival in which the rustic population around Naples celebrated at once the glories of spring and a liturgical event. Religious and pagan ritual were joined in this picture which was far more ambitious than Robert's smaller paintings, like the *Girl of Procida*, which were made for private sale. Indeed, the *Madonna dell'Arco* set the stage for the elevation of peasant genre to the level of Salon history painting.

The apogee of a classical peasant genre painting in France came at the Salon of 1831 in which there were major peasant images by Robert, Schnetz, Haudebourt-Lescot, and Horace Vernet. Vernet's *Peasant Woman of Ariccia* was compared in contemporary criticism to Raphael. Schnetz's *Peasant Family Caught by a Sudden Overflow of the Tiber Escaping through the Waters* depicted a family of *contadini* confronting the elements with an emotional intensity and courage derived from earlier history paintings and was admired for what one reviewer called its "classical air." Madame Haudebourt-Lescot contributed a *Popular Festival in the Neighbourhood of Rome* which was considered, wrongly, to be the first major painting to represent a naïve scene of popular customs in Italy. And finally there was Léopold Robert, whose *Harvesters Arriving in the Pontine Marshes* was the success of the 1831 Salon. Robert's painting was hailed as an indisputable masterpiece, a "géorgique en peinture" evoking at once classical bas-relief, the beautiful heads of Raphael's Madonnas, and the learned poses of Poussin. At one stroke Robert linked classical civilization in ancient Rome, Renaissance Italy, and France in the Golden Age with the naïve gestures and costumes of the Italian peasantry.

Jean-Victor Schnetz (1787-1870):
Vow to the Madonna, 1831.

Who were these "peasants" to whom Robert and his followers paid such homage? Who were the models for the dancers in the *Madonna dell'Arco* and the countryfolk in the *Harvesters Arriving in the Pontine Marshes*? Not surprisingly, they were not peasants at all, but rather the handsomest people chosen from a group of brigands rounded up by French forces between Naples and Rome in 1819. These brigands were visited by Robert, Schnetz, and Michallon almost immediately after their capture and imprisonment at Termini. Several of them, notably the excitable and beautiful Maria Grazia and her sister Teresina, were painted by countless artists who made their pilgrimage to the environs of Rome in the wake of Robert's success. Indeed, Maria Grazia told the French novelist Edmond About as late as 1860 that "I posed in my costume a thousand times and more, and they told me that my portrait was in the churches and palaces of your country."

What do we learn of the peasantry and Italian peasant life from these French paintings of the 1820s? We learn a great deal about clothing or costume and about the particularity of certain "peasant" physiognomies borrowed from the brigands. We learn also that peasants were both devout and joyous, and that they presided benignly over a landscape which, according to one fervent English travel writer of the late nineteenth century, "contains no point which does not make a picture." We learn of festivals and celebrations which greeted the seasons and counterbalanced the work of the fields.

This collective "portrait," for it was in many senses a portrait, was an idealized one, and it was intended to be. But what is remarkable about these classical images of "real" peasants is the extent of their departure from the truth of peasant life during the nineteenth century. Fortunately we have witnesses other than Schnetz and Robert to tell us about the Italian peasantry they pictured. After the peace of 1815, French, German, and English travellers, the men and women whom one writer called "les âmes passionnées du Nord," flocked to Italy and created what came to be an "Age d'Or" for foreigners. The Italy which they sought, an Italy of monuments and works of art, was in reality the native land of a people who lived in misery and poverty. Indeed, the Italian peasantry, particularly in the neighbourhood of Rome, was among the poorest and most disease-ridden in Europe. When one looks at Robert's *Harvesters Arriving*, one must remember that most viewers saw the Roman Campagna as the seat of a long-past civilization fallen into ruin and poverty. The Reverend John Eustace, on what he called his "classical" tour through Italy in the mid-1830s, found "the appearance of the few peasants that inhabit the Campagna frightful and disgusting; bloated bellies, distorted features, dark yellow complexion, livid eyes and lips; in short, all the symptoms of dropsy, jaundice, and ague seem united in their persons." George Evans, a self-styled "classicist and connoisseur" in Italy during the first half of the 1830s, complained as he travelled through the country about "depopulation, dying peasants, wretched villages, and miserable hovels." Finally, he "caught the first glimpse of Rome and, at Monte Rosi, entered the bleak and desolate Campagna."

Even when one entered the city of Rome itself, one was greeted by an enormous population of impoverished and homeless peasants turned beggars and brigands, those whom Edmond About accurately called "les paysans de Rome." This population had existed for centuries and been depicted thousands of times both as staffage figures in seventeenth-century Roman landscapes and as main figures in the genre paintings of the so-called Bamboccianti. Yet these straggling beggars and ill-clad but picturesque maidens at fountains scarcely prepare us for the paintings of Schnetz, Robert, and Haudebourt-Lescot. The grandest images of these urban "peasants" painted in the first half of the nineteenth century are the peasant worshippers of which Schnetz's *Vow to the Madonna* of 1831 is the most famous example. Schnetz's painting represents a family of handsome, sturdy peasants who have travelled to Rome to plead with an almost unseen Madonna for the cure of their ailing son. One feels the futility of their cause, especially when one knows the disease-ridden status of so many Italian peasants. Their efforts are intended to move us, perhaps to tears, in sympathy not only for their personal plight, but for that of their class. Again, Schnetz's image of peasant piety in an urban context departs radically from written accounts of such scenes. Hippolyte Taine was at St Peter's for Easter in 1864 and described the

peasant worshippers in his *Voyage en Italie* of 1866: "Their costumes are strange: old sheepskin or goatskin jackets, leather gaiters, bluish cloaks a hundred times soaked with rain, and sandals of hide as in primitive times; the stench of all this is unbearable. Their staring eyes glow like those of an animal; even more glowing and wilder are those of the women, sallow and shrunken by fever."

It is important, when analysing these French pictures of an idealized classical peasantry in the 1820s and 1830s, to remember that the French were not alone in the creation of such images and that they cannot be explained solely as solutions to the problem of proper subjects for French Salon painting. Of the German Nazarenes, Overbeck painted several idealized peasant pictures, and his *Vittoria Caldoni of Albano* of 1821 can be compared with the numerous single female peasants portrayed by Robert, Schnetz, and Vernet. Unlike Robert's *Girl of Procida* of 1822, Overbeck's *Vittoria Caldoni* is shown in the context of peasant work, resting in the shade of an old oak amidst a sea of grain which becomes the sea itself. Having dropped her scythe, she sits protectively on the bundle of lunch which she has carried to the fields. Melons and a conspicuous apple allude to both her fertility and her link with the biblical Eve, and the plants surrounding her abound in further allegorical meanings. Although beautiful, she is not seductive. She looks at us with a melancholy gravity, far from the gentle coquetry of Robert's *Girl of Procida*. She is idealized, but not in the same way or for the same audience as the peasants of the French painters of Italian genre. The moralism and high-mindedness of German painting in Rome during the first half of the nineteenth century is always present in their paintings of Italian peasants. Speckter's *Portrait of a Woman of Albano* of 1831 has none of the French fascination with exact ethnography in its costume or setting. The drapery of his female peasant evokes not only that of the classical past, but also the weighty folds of Michelangelo's draped figures. This woman of Albano is more a sibyl than a peasant.

Erwin Speckter (1806-1835):
Portrait of a Woman of Albano, 1831.

Friedrich Overbeck (1789-1869):
Vittoria Caldoni of Albano, 1821.

It is clear, however, from a comparision of these German paintings of Italian peasants with those of their French contemporaries, that similarities abound. Johann Ender's *Italian Women Pilgrims* of 1847 has the gravity and stability of an Overbeck or a Speckter, but is concerned primarily with costume description and peasant religiousness. The piety of Italian peasants appealed as much to Catholic Bavaria and Austria as it did to the traditional religion of the post-revolutionary monarchy in France. Both the Germans and French stressed the particularity of peasant individuals in their paintings. Robert represented a very real Italian girl in 1822, while Overbeck's title gives us the name of his model and Speckter called his painting a portrait. Each group of artists used the same population of models, and each placed their peasants in manifold idealized settings with pose associations and symbolic references no less sophisticated than those used by history painters. As a result, their images hover inconclusively between the realism of their models, props, and even genre events, and the artificial-

ity of their compositions and historical references. As such, they speak equally to a Europe after the cataclysm of Napoleon, anxious at once for novelty and for continuity, and it is no accident that the first sustained investigation of "contemporary" people in the context of high art focused not on the peasantry or urban proletariat of France or Germany, but on the "classical" peasantry of Italy. Somehow, Italian reality was ideal by definition, no matter how degraded it had become in fact. Travel writers, sceptical and truthful as a rule, tending more often than not to exaggerate the negative qualities of foreign places in contrast to those at home, had not the necessity for such idealism. It is to lyric and epic poets, the anxious Romantics of England, France, and Germany, that one must look for comparisons.

Classical painting of the Italian peasantry did not end in northern Europe with the tragic suicide of Robert in Venice in 1835. Indeed, French painting of the middle and later nineteenth century made notable contributions to the international tradition which began in Rome

Johann Ender (1793-1854):
Italian Women Pilgrims, 1847.

Camille Corot (1796-1875):
Agostina, 1866.

around 1820. A visitor to the Paris Salon, even as late as the mid-century, could see as many Italian landscapes and peasants as he did those of his native France, and the flow of such images by no means stopped with the rise of regionalism and the so-called national schools of art. Not only did travel books devoted to Italy and illustrated with peasant figures in regional costumes appear in profusion throughout the nineteenth century, but reproductive prints of entire compositions and selected figures by Schnetz and Robert flooded the market in the 1830s and early 1840s.

The greatest artist in this tradition, the one who carried classical peasant painting to new heights, was Camille Corot. Born in 1796, only two years after Robert, Corot outlived his contemporary by forty years and painted costumed Italian "peasants" until his death in 1875. For Corot, Italy was more an imaginative than an actual home. Although he made three trips, each was brief, and he seems to have preferred Italy at a distance. His first journey, was made in 1825–1828 in the company of the young French landscape painter F. E. Bertin, and most of his Italian pictures of the 1820s and 1830s are landscape and architectural studies. His few Italian figures are straightforward, even awkward, general studies of the pose, drapery, and costume of humble models in regional dress and were not intended to be exhibited. In contrast to the painted studies of single figures by artists like Michallon and Robert, Corot generalized his treatment of the costumes and was more interested in effect than accuracy. Strangely, it was not until the last two decades of his life, after his final trip in 1843, that Corot turned in earnest to the "noble" peasant figures of Italy and produced a body of single figure paintings of Italian peasant women which are among the great achievements of the century. In some of them, like *Agostina*, Corot portrayed the Italian model in front of an appropriate "native" landscape. In others, like the *Italian Girl*, the figure appears against the undifferentiated wall of his atelier. Careful study of his late Italian peasant figures reveals that the costumes are idiosyncratic and unlike those represented in

Camille Corot (1796-1875):
Italian Girl, 1871-1872.

costume books or earlier paintings. Corot seems to have obtained them from the Paris theatres rather than Italy and, as in his early peasant costume studies, reveals himself to be more interested in broad allusions to the Italian rural woman than in the facts of her costume or setting. Like many of his late Italian landscapes, these figures are "rêves d'Italie," even farther from reality than the Salon pictures of Robert and Schnetz. Their primary quality is melancholy and listlessness. Far from the suffering realm of real Italian peasants, they are equally distant from the dancing and celebration of Robert's rural Italy. It is to the world of the ballet and the theatre which Corot loved and to the pastoral poetry of French academic poets at mid-century that one looks for comparison. Where Robert placed the Italian peasant confidently in the Paris Salon, Corot, whose pictures were also exhibited at the Salons, created dream-filled worlds for a nation suffering severely from the "mal du siècle," the disease of modernism. His peasant women, and they are always women, speak sadly to us from an Italy which never existed. He meant them to evoke a gentle pastoral age.

Corot followed an isolated path of his own, borrowing from Schnetz and Robert only their subjects and their idealizing tendency. It was Bouguereau who became the true inheritor of the Italian peasant images which were so successful in the Salons of the 1830s. Trained as a history painter, Bouguereau made only one trip to Italy, in 1850, on which he seems to have painted more landscapes than rural figures. By the 1870s, however, he was well on the way to becoming the major Salon painter of classical rural figures and, like Corot, he expanded his repertoire to include French peasants. In style and treatment of the subject, his paintings, whether of Italian or French peasants, follow the lead of Robert, Schnetz, and Haudebourt-Lescot. The *Donkey Ride* of 1878 is almost a direct remaking in simpler form of Robert's "succès de Salon," *Harvesters Arriving in the Pontine Marshes*. Yet, while Robert attempted to combine accuracy of observation with the visual rhetoric of history painting, Bouguereau was less interested in actuality. While Robert included male and female labourers, no labourers appear in Bouguereau's allegorical harvest and, as in the paintings of Corot, he used generically Italian costumes, preferring not to be precise about the local origins of his figures.

Bouguereau approached Robert more closely in a painting called *The Rest*. In it, a Raphaelesque mother and her two children are juxtaposed against a distant view of St Peter's Basilica. Although Catholic only on his father's side, Bouguereau clearly wanted to project an image of Italian rural piety not fundamentally different from Robert or Schnetz. His peasant woman and children rest rather than work, and they rest in a holy landscape at once classical and religious in its meanings. This landscape with its beautiful and pious inhabitants can be contrasted in an interesting way with Bouguereau's French peasant images. In the latter, the female figures tend to be erotic young women, alone or in pairs, placed so that they look longingly at their male viewers. The Italian peasant women are more chaste and embody the values of high civilization. They teach rather than titillate.

A complete characterization of classical peasant imagery must include the now obscure French painter Ernest Hébert. A cousin of

William Bouguereau (1825-1905):
The Donkey Ride (Return from the Harvest), 1878.

William Bouguereau (1825-1905):
The Rest (Mother and Children), 1879.

Stendhal and an artist of great intelligence, Hébert painted Italian peasant genre throughout the 1850s, filling the void between Robert and Corot. Although idealized in form and placed in refined, even classical, figural groupings, his peasant images are far from the idealized Italian peasants of Robert, Schnetz, and even the later Bouguereau. His first great Salon picture was painted in a certain opposition to Robert, whose friend Schnetz was by this time the director of the French Academy in Rome. Hébert's *Malaria*, exhibited at the Salon of 1851, dealt frankly and simply with the disease of the Roman peasantry which had been observed by countless travel writers. The setting is the Pontine Marshes, the same as that portrayed in the background of Robert's triumphant *Harvesters Arriving*. Henry Roujon, an early biographer of Hébert, recorded what he called the young Hébert's last view of this landscape: "On his way back to Rome by Terracina, he had crossed the Pontine Marshes. There, in that accursed and dismal spot, Italy had bidden him farewell. In his last look back at the land of happiness, he had glimpsed a cruel vision. He wished to translate into beauty what the fever-stricken regions of Italy had revealed to him of her secret." Hébert shows us a "barque de la mort" travelling on the mosquito-infested

Ernest Hébert (1817-1908):
Malaria, c. 1851.

swamps around Rome. The figures possess no energy, no life; even the standing male peasant who seems to guide the boat leans limply on his pole.

This deathly landscape with its exquisitely arranged figures must be seen in relation to his *Women of Cervara at the Fountain,* Hébert's Salon painting of 1859. This quasi-erotic image represents two women and a child in the village of Cervara, in the hill country west of Rome, a village noted for its brigandry and rarely visited by foreigners. Théophile Gautier was perhaps the first to recognize not only the beauty, but also the difficult mystery of Hébert's painting. "The antique elegance of the pose is admirably rhythmed and sings out one of those melodies of line to which any artist's eye is responsive... The figures have the true historical dimensions, and the character of the picture is at once rude and delicate, tender and fierce, motionless and passionate, all to the strangest effect." Gautier was of course correct. For, in spite of the allusions to the antique with which Hébert, like his predecessors and followers, imbued his figures, the painting possesses more of a mysterious aura of degenerate beauty than one might at first glance notice. These are not the joyous, religious Italian peasants of the 1820s and 1830s. These wasted figures inhabit the landscape of "sadness, melancholy, and desolation" so often described by nineteenth-century travel writers.

Unlike any other nineteenth-century painter of Italian peasant life, Hébert managed to join fact and symbol and to create beautifully coherent, classically constructed pictures which conveyed the realities of peasant life in the Campagna. Unlike Robert, who used brigands as models for peasants, Hébert painted his brigands as brigands. Unlike Schnetz who represented disease only in connection with the cure which religion brings, Hébert recognized the reality of death in the Campagna. It is perhaps fitting to the emotional intentions of Hébert's despairing image to juxtapose it with a quotation from Thomas Roscoe's *The Tourist in Italy,* published in 1831. "Over this wild waste no rural dwelling, nor scattered hamlets, nor fields, nor gardens were to be seen... All was ruin... but it is melancholy... to behold an immense tract of fertile land in the immediate vicinity of one of the greatest cities in the world, pestilent with disease and death... Amidst the fearful loneliness and stillness of this scene of desolation, as we advanced through the long dreary tract that divided us from Rome, a few wretched peasants, whose looks bespoke them victims of slow, consuming disease, occasionally reminded us of the tremendous ravage of human life which this invisible and mysterious power is annually making."

It is no accident that these "ravages of human life" were left unpictured until the time of Hébert. The progressive and moralizing function of art was so profoundly felt in the early decades of the nineteenth century, and so closely associated with Italy and classical civilization, that no earlier artist had awakened to the powerful poetry of death in rural Italy. Perhaps guided by the increasing "mal du siècle" which became such a dominating characteristic of French intellectual life at mid-century, Hébert was moved to paint what was in the end to be a premature adieu to Italy. *Malaria* is, after all, a painting which owes a profound debt in its meaning, if not its form, to Romanticism, and the Romanticism of despair and dejection was the predominant French Romanticism of the so-called generation of 1830. In these ways, Hébert's picture prepares us for Realism, and his disease-ridden peasants are both beautiful and classical without being ideal.

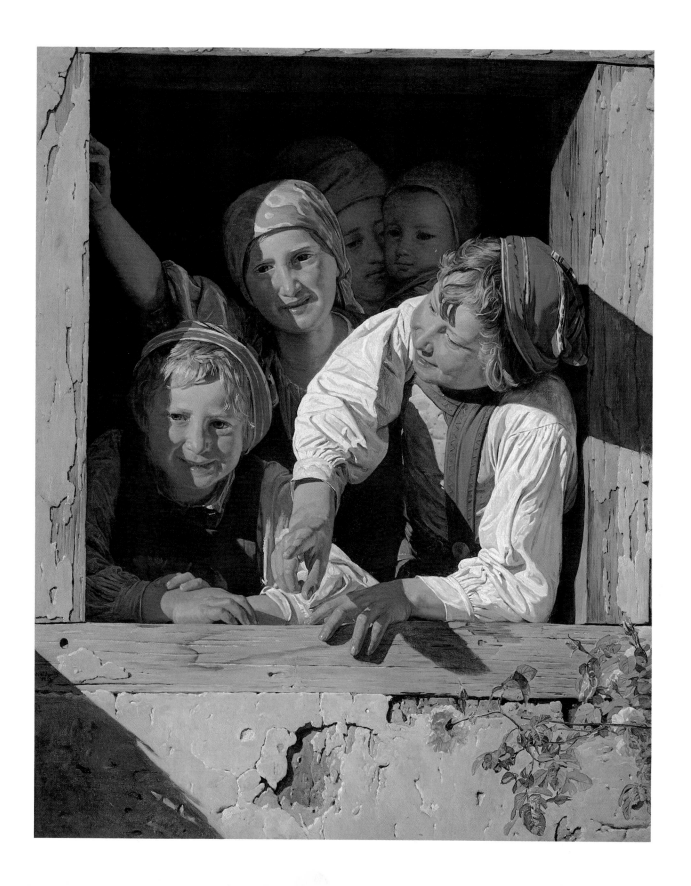

THE RISE OF REALISM:

The Northern Peasant, 1840-1900

Soon after the death of Robert, European painters began to turn their attention in earnest to the rural populations of their own countries. By the early 1840s, an increasing number of German rural images made their appearance, and in the last years of that decade the Paris Salon was to house important paintings representing French in addition to Italian peasants. If Italian peasants were appropriate vehicles to carry various meanings to the public, then it seemed only a matter of time before such meanings were attached equally to their northern counterparts. However, the road to a true pan-European peasant painting was not an easy one, and there were many reasons why the images were at first resisted. Painting, of all the arts, was considered the most noble in its aims, and for most Europeans there was little nobility in peasant life. Yet, with the steady increase in scientific naturalism, the continued fascination with "savages" from abroad, and the growth of ethnographically motivated travel books and collections of folk tales and folk costumes, the cultural meanings of the northern peasant began to expand as well. If he was not exactly the noble savage of the eighteenth century, the northern peasant came to be seen, in certain circles at least, as the closest of all European men to nature. It was, however, this very connection with nature which disturbed so many nineteenth-century viewers and critics because, in spite of the fact that artists including David and Valenciennes rooted their new aesthetic in

Ferdinand Waldmüller (1793-1865):
Children at the Window, 1853.

studies from life, nature as a concept had been generally considered as the antithesis of art, or at least high art, for many generations in Europe. Early painters of the northern peasantry accordingly placed themselves in an ambivalent position between "art" and "nature," and their images record their struggles to surmount this ambivalence.

At an early date in these struggles, the German artist Jacob Becker painted a superbly dramatic scene of peasant genre, the *Shepherd Struck by Lightning*. This large painting with amply proportioned figures represents a lightning storm in rural Germany which has just struck a group of oak trees and the shepherd standing beneath them. Nearby peasants, who had been harvesting in the fields, run to the aid of the dying man as his sheep bleat and the thunderstorm rages on. The picture strikes us today as an uneasy compromise between the emotional intensity and morality of earlier history paintings representing dying heroes or kings and the sober depiction of actual peasant life in modern Germany. Becker has been exacting in his details. The costumes are precisely rendered,

and the faces and hands of the figures carefully observed from particular models. Yet the ensemble is calculated to impress us, by reference to standard pictorial types, with the relentless forces of nature and the sternness of fate. Peasants, so we learn, as well as heroes, can die by the hand of God. In this particular case, the peasant figures serve to generalize the meaning of the painting, to make the moral posture relevant to the broadest base of society. For the viewer of this dramatic scene, the peasant becomes a kind of Everyman, the most basic of human beings. So the painting is not to be read as a scene from the daily life of a group of peasants in Germany; it teaches us as little about their lives as Robert, Schnetz, Overbeck, or Speckter taught us about the Italian peasant in the 1820s and 1830s. Becker was not alone, however, in his choice of German peasants as proper subjects for painting. His contemporary, Ferdinand Waldmüller, had already begun by 1840 to make his mark as a painter of rural genre in his native Austria, and he would become the major painter of rural life in that country until his death in 1865.

Jacob Becker (1810-1872):
Shepherd Struck by Lightning, 1844.

Trained at the Vienna Academy, first with the Viennese flower painter Zintler and later in the ateliers of Maurer and Lampi, Waldmüller eventually became the keeper of the Vienna Picture Gallery and later a professor at the Academy. But after 1840 he began to oppose the traditional academic teaching of art, advocating instead studies "made from nature." The growth of Waldmüller's peasant genre is interesting to observe because, unlike Becker's, his oeuvre is both large and well documented. The problems involved in the early depictions of northern peasants can be elucidated by a comparison between two paintings by Waldmüller.

His *Young Peasant Woman with Three Children in a Window,* of 1840, brought the northern peasant to a level of pictorial reality almost unprecedented in the history of art. The young peasant mother, actually the painter's wife, with her (and their) three young children look directly at the viewer from an open window in a rustic rural dwelling. The window frame is carefully painted to become, by analogy, the picture frame, but we look not outwards to a natural landscape, but inwards to a darkened human realm. The style keeps to the standards of surface finish, balanced composition, control of contour, and geometric idealization of human form which were omnipresent in the classical peasant image. There are, however, two basic factors which separate the painting from these earlier and "higher" expressions. First, it represents Austrian peasants with no pretensions to classical lineage and, second, it "presents" them to the viewer with a frank directness which, to a large extent, denies the Raphaelesque pictorial rhetoric of the painter's style. We, the viewer, become "real" and the painting forces us to accept *it* as real by confronting us. Perhaps we are a visitor who has knocked at the window of a peasant house to inquire for directions. Perhaps, more radically, we are ourselves a peasant, the father of the children who has come home from the fields. Our identity is ambiguous but our presence is evoked with an utter directness of gaze and gesture.

Ferdinand Waldmüller (1793-1865):
Young Peasant Woman with Three Children in a Window, 1840.

Achille Michallon (1797-1822):
Peasant Woman of the Roman Countryside.

intensely saturated and even vulgar by comparison. While before the figures had been confined to their darkened interior world, now they burst out vigorously into the space of the viewer with its rotting wood, crumbling plaster, and inexplicable shadows. The energy and vitality of the later picture suggest that it was translated directly from nature rather than constructed, that it represents an actual moment in a highly unstable, active time. The mother, whose Raphaelesque presence had anchored and stabilized the earlier painting, now stands in the darkness of the background clutching her youngest child to her body and looking not at us, but wistfully down, as if in another world. The stable bond between mother and children which before had been the subject gives way to an exploration of adolescence, as the children move gradually beyond the protective interior of their mother into the hard light of the out-of-doors. Waldmüller's later painting, one of the greatest of his career, accepts utterly its peasant subject and makes use of peasant costumes and a minimal, but believable, rural setting, to explore larger questions of the growth and generation of modern family life. Perhaps because of the directness and human relevance of his subject, Waldmüller attempted to break down the manifold barriers between viewer and picture which had characterized the vast majority of earlier paintings of European peasants. As in the case of Becker, the Austrian peasant became for Waldmüller a pictorial Everyman, enabling the painter to enter the lives and emotions of every viewer.

It is tempting to connect this new "realism" with the depiction of the northern, unclassical peasant. Yet any close or sympathetic reading of either classical or northern peasants suggests that this is not the case. There are many paintings, especially those of religious and family scenes (Waldmüller's *Harvest* and Millet's *Angelus*, see pages 97 and 100), in which northern peasants are as idealized as the classical peasants of Robert or Overbeck. In addition, there are converse images of Italian peasants whose realism is decidedly anti-

Several years later, in 1853, when Waldmüller remade the composition using the same models at a different window in interestingly analogous poses, the style changed dramatically. Where the earlier version presents its subjects in a beautifully modulated range of values, light in the later one breaks across the window and the figures with an almost violent brilliance. Dark shadows cut through the faces of the two children to the left, making a clear reading of their heads as single volumes difficult, if not impossible. Where the earlier palette is subdued and golden, the later one is

Johann Hasselhorst (1825-1904):
Old Italian Peasant.

Friedrich Wasmann (1805-1886):
Seated Italian Peasant Woman with Spindle, 1832.

classical. In each of these small paintings by Michallon, Hasselhorst, and Wasmann, the figure contours are ungraceful and energetic, zigzagging in and out of the painted ground. In each, the folds and fittings of the costumes are clearly observed from nature rather than calculated to serve some symbolic or compositional function. Although it must be remembered that these three proto-realist sketches were made only for private study and were not considered by their makers to be works of art in their own right, they *do* form part of a process of pictorial preparation rooted absolutely in natural observation. Indeed, Robert at times kept closely to the real and, if it was Courbet who said that "the only history worth painting is contemporary history," such surely was the aim of Robert and his contemporaries.

Not until almost twenty years after Robert's famous Salon of 1831 did another group of peasant images, this time with French subjects, challenge the standards of Salon painting. The Salon of 1850 contained several masterpieces of peasant genre including *The Sower* painted by a Norman artist of peasant life, J. F. Millet, and Gustave Courbet's immense canvas *Peasants of Flagey Returning from the Fair.* Each of these paintings was regarded as absolutely realist, concerned, that is, with the reproduction of the

Jean-François Millet (1814-1875):
The Sower, 1850.

world seen and experienced by the painter. Each was thought to be crude and vulgar because of both its style and its subject. It is important, however, in evaluating peasant imagery as such, to consider these works of art in terms of the conventions laid down by earlier painters of peasants. Millet's sower was a more revolutionary subject than Courbet's enormous multi-figural genre scene. Like many paintings by Courbet, the *Peasants of Flagey* exists as a kind of corrective to previous paintings, in this case Robert's *Harvesters Arriving* and *Madonna dell'Arco*. Like Robert, Courbet chose a grand moment in the lives of his rural population, a moment connected with a rural fair to which peasants went to exchange their goods and celebrate in their best regional costumes. Like Robert, Courbet was concerned about the details of individual figures and the niceties of their dress. Yet, where Robert stresses the natural gracefulness and gaiety of the peasants, Courbet created a leaden procession of heavily painted figures moving unsteadily back home. He was careful to make clear the levels of rural

society, from the "seigneur" on horseback to the peasant women walking behind them with bundles on their heads. All the figures, except the two horsemen, are self-absorbed and hence isolated from the collective experience chosen by the painter. They walk, rather like the animals they follow, with a stolid determination under the waning sky of eastern France. It is the picture's frank acceptance of these negative values, its complement of pictorial and social discontinuities, and its woodenness of treatment that made it the "succès de scandale" at the Salon of 1850. Taking on Robert and the entire classical tradition of Italian peasant painting with a grim determination, Courbet created an image as imposing as that of his predecessor, but certainly not as ennobling.

Millet's now famous painting of a solitary rural worker sowing the seed for a future harvest at dawn is tied less insistently to tradition than Courbet's immense realist "machine." The figure of the sower has few individual features; he is simply a rural labourer, and his work clothes have none of the complexity and charm of a

peasant costume. It is, rather, the rhythm of his body silhouetted against the early morning sky that lends a dance-like energy to the picture. Interestingly, *The Sower* is the first major peasant image we have considered which represents the work of the fields itself. Millet's peasants—and he was to become the greatest painter of peasant life in the history of art—are always at work. There are no arrivals or departures from festivals and fairs. There are no joyful worshipping scenes in Paris or even in the country churches of northern France. His one great moment of rural piety occurs at the end of a long day in the fields before the peasants trudge home to prepare supper.

These two French paintings reveal the varieties of expression within the canons of realism and make it clear that the peasant image, even in one country at one time, was not a unified, easily comprehensible one. Courbet explored the tension among social classes in the rural world and juxtaposed his peasants with figures from higher social stations. Millet, on the other hand, omitted all but peasants from his paintings and stressed the grand organizing cycle of seasonal work in both the fields and barnyards of northern France. Courbet's realism shares with that of Robert a particularizing quality, an interest in the individual figure and details of costume and accessories. Millet, on the other hand, chose to generalize his figures and created several often-repeated peasant types (page 36).

In confronting the realism of these two artists, one confronts for the first time in the history of peasant genre painting artists who represented a rural world in which they were born and spent much of their lives. Millet was the son of a peasant farmer, born in a small thatched farmhouse near the desolate coast of Normandy. He spent his life first in Normandy, then briefly in Paris, and finally in the fields and forests near the village of Barbizon south-east of Paris. In a letter to his biographer, Alfred Sensier, Millet called himself a "peasant of peasants," living always among them in villages and hamlets, tending his own vegetable garden. Courbet, on the other hand, was born in the provincial town of Ornans in the Franche-Comté to a family best described

Jean-François Millet (1814-1875):
Woman Pasturing her Cow, 1858.

Jean-François Millet (1814-1875):
The Potato Harvest, 1854-1857.

as provincial bourgeoisie. But because of its size and position within an enfolding valley Ornans provided the young Courbet with direct access to wild and forested country with rivers, cliffs, and grottoes, as well as hill-top villages and peasant fields. Unlike Millet's villages, Ornans was a stratified town and the painter was made easily aware of its social barriers. As a result of this, as well as of the increased politicization both of Courbet and the entire north-east of France, his rural images possess an insistently social quality. They gnaw at the traditions of society, and hence, for Courbet, the peasant is seen in the context of all society and not as an isolated "natural" man.

In 1855 a young painter from the Pas-de-Calais, Jules Breton, submitted to the Salon a major peasant genre composition, *The Gleaners*. It came in the wake of peasant images by Breton's heroes, Courbet and, to a much greater extent, Millet, whose work he had seen and admired in the Salons of the early 1850s. With his *Gleaners*, Breton commenced a long and distinguished career both as a painter of French peasant genre and as a writer of prose and poetry. In spite of recent attempts to revive interest in his work, Breton's paintings have been dismissed by three generations of critics and historians of advanced French painting as insipid and sentimental pictorial accounts of peasant life in northern France during the second half of the nineteenth century. This view is unjust, and a careful examination of Breton's major canvases reveals a painter of talent, one who understood French peasants in ways different from Millet or Courbet. *The Gleaners* represents more than forty peasant figures arranged in complex, pictorially unprecedented groupings in an immense field near the village of Marlotte at twilight. Mostly women and children, they are bent at the task of picking the remnants from an already harvested field under the baneful supervision of an armed and uniformed man. Rather like Waldmüller, Breton chose to represent the figures in an angled, raking light which breaks over the folds and wrinkles of their humble working clothes,

36

increasing the amount of visual incidence and lending specificity to the scene. The image is highly complex and filled with information about social hierarchy, rural charity, seasonal labour, costumes, and specific work-oriented poses. It accepts the difficult ambivalence of its subject with a frankness and moral detachment not often found in large-scale Salon painting. Yet, in certain ways, its very moral ambivalence was to be avoided in the future by Breton, who turned increasingly towards subjects of abundance and rural piety.

Seen as a whole population, Breton's peasants are strong individuals. They work communally and are most often healthy and young. Their work is hard and real, but never thankless. The contrast with Millet's peasants who can stagger across the fields with faggots loaded on their backs, "bowed by the weight of centuries," is superficially great. Yet the antithesis Breton-Ideal/Millet-Real is exaggerated. Millet's peasants appear in a variety of idealized

settings. They conform to poses derived from Renaissance religious pictures; they sit in rooms which suggest Vermeer and other seventeenth-century Dutch painters of interior genre; they often derive from portal sculpture or low-life scenes by Bruegel. Their reality is not contemporary. They do not, like Courbet's rural workers, occupy an important place in the politics of art. Their intention is ahistorical; they depict the human condition or, as Millet himself put it, "the indispensable and necessary bond" between man and man as well as man and nature. Both Millet's peasants and those of Breton fill a long, habitual stretch of time, a time which has no meaning in terms of the struggles of armies, the whims of fashion, and the machinations of politics. Millet and Breton, in spite of their apparent differences in artistic alliance, attempted to transcend modernity by painting peasants not as they existed in the post-revolutionary upheavals, not as members of the over-populated, ignorant, insular class described by

Balzac, Marx, Engels, and Renan, but as basic human beings untouched by urban, industrial civilization. The rhetoric of this position is of course late Romantic. One can easily think of precedents in English and continental Romanticism and in the search for origins, for basic man, which formed a stream of French thinking after Rousseau. Although Breton indulged in sentimentality much more than Millet, the intentions of his art vis-à-vis society, especially urban society, were nearly the same.

There were many minor realist painters of peasant life in France, most of whom are forgotten today. Two, at least, have retained a status roughly equivalent to that of Breton: Jules Bastien-Lepage and Léon Lhermitte. Born in Lorraine, Bastien-Lepage came of a small peasant proprietor family. Although he studied at the Ecole des Beaux-Arts, he was critical of the training he received, commenting to one of his biographers that he did not understand why a man should imitate old pictures and paint gods and goddesses or Greeks and Romans he knew nothing about. His solution was different: "One would return home, to Brittany or Gascony, Lorraine or Normandy, one would quietly paint one's native place, and when one morning after reading a book one felt like painting the Prodigal Son or Priam at the feet of Achilles, or something similar, one would imagine the scene without stale memories of the museum, in a local setting with such models as happened to be at hand, as if the old drama had occurred the day before. In this way one would be able to quicken one's art with true life, to make it beautiful and touching for everyone. I am bending all my efforts in this direction."

All of Bastien-Lepage's larger and more important rural genre pictures (see for example page 82) were painted in his native Lorraine, with local peasants as models; in his most famous "history painting" the figure of Joan of Arc (page 97) is based on real peasants from his "coin de terre" rather than professional models. For Bastien-Lepage, everything in nature was capable of being "portrayed," and this he did to such an extent that one critic, an admirer of

Millet, called him a "photographic copyist" whose work was merely reportorial and uninterpreted. Yet, at the height of his short-lived career, Bastien-Lepage was pursued by lesser artists wishing to learn his techniques, and his pictures were the great successes of the Salon in the late 1870s and early 1880s.

Just before his death, Bastien-Lepage was working with his biographer André Theuriet on a publication to be called *Les Mois Rustiques*. The project was completed by Theuriet with the help of the painter and printmaker Léon Lhermitte, whom Theuriet himself called a "maître peintre des mœurs rustiques." This was one of several such collaborations for Lhermitte, whose work probably reached a wider audience than that of any other artist of peasant life during the latter half of the nineteenth century. While most of Lhermitte's energies were devoted to drawing and printmaking (Van Gogh described him as the Millet and Breton of black and white), he did paint a number of major canvases dealing with rural subjects—mostly of rural labour. His *Harvesters' Wages* of 1882 (see page 120) carried the visual realism of Bastien-Lepage into a realm of sociological realism founded not simply on the study of peasant figures, but on a knowledge of contemporary peasant life.

Although the French peasant, both as image and as fact, has been widely studied, it would be wrong to restrict the peasant image to that great nation. It is true that Paris was the art capital of Europe throughout the nineteenth century and that peasant painting had its major locus at the Paris Salon. But it was widespread and answered similar needs in other countries. Norway showered fame and success on Adolph Tidemand, an artist trained in Düsseldorf and Rome who became what one early historian of nineteenth-century art called "the Léopold Robert of the North." After 1845 he turned his attention to the rural inhabitants of Norway, painting the solemn and idyllic peasants and fishermen of his native land with an interest in costume, precise portraiture, and ethnographically focused scenes of work, festivals, and religion. In Austria, Waldmüller was at the centre of a large group of peasant genre painters bent on a new "national" expression based on the study of rural life. In Sweden there was Hugo Salmson; in Germany, Liebermann, Leibl, Defregger, and a host of others. In the Low Countries the young Van Gogh and Jozef Israels specialized in the depiction of peasant life. In Czechoslovakia Josef Mánes founded a national school of peasant painters in 1849, and in Warsaw the Academy itself encouraged a nationalistic rural realism. William Morris Hunt took French realist peasant genre even to America. What had been started by a few hardy European artists in the 1840s and codified in the Paris Salon in the early 1850s was to be a worldwide movement during the second half of the nineteenth century, when the peasant became the most widely painted class of people in Europe.

Peasant realism moved in two directions. The first was towards portraiture and individualization of peasants; the second, towards genre and carefully observed peasant types pictured in their own homes and fields. Each method had its roots in the two kinds of peasant painting inaugurated by Robert and Schnetz, the single figure study for sale and the large, multifigural scene for exhibition.

Peasant portraits hover inconclusively between the generic and the individual, as can be seen from three divergent examples painted at different times in three different countries (pages 39-40). They usually bear generic titles, and we are rarely allowed access to the name, home, or particular circumstances of the peasant portrayed. In all three examples, as in most peasant portraits, the artist excluded accessories and focused his attention on the head, upper torso, or hands. Character is communicated by the facial features and certain minimal information conveyed by the position of the head and the relationship between the figure and the compositional format. Tidemand's portrait is a simple presentation of a middle-aged male peasant from Voss made in July 1855. Straggling hairs and accidental folds and wrinkles are carefully rendered. As with all realist

Adolph Tidemand (1814-1876):
Peasant from Voss, 1855.

Wilhelm Leibl (1844-1900):
Girl with a White Kerchief, 1875-1877.

images, the figure is presented as he was on a particular day in a particular place. Leibl, in his brilliant portrait of a *Girl with White Kerchief* painted in the mid 1870s, activates his sitter, who looks sidelong at us as if she has just turned her head. She is young and attractive, but neither beautiful nor idealized, and we believe utterly in her individuality although we will never know her name. It is her relationship to the non-peasant viewer which interests Leibl, and she is not "presented" for our analysis as is Tidemand's male portrait. Van Gogh, in his fine peasant portraits of the 1880s, reverted to the direct posture used by Tidemand, although the frontal and symmetrical position of the head and headdress of the peasant woman makes her almost a devotional image. Unlike Tidemand and Leibl, Van Gogh painted broadly, almost crudely, in a manner analogous to the crudeness of his subject, and there is an intense pathos and humanity in the expression of this anonymous peasant woman. Each of these peasant figures has a forceful presence as an individual in ways

William D. McKay (1844-1923):
Field Working in Spring:
At the Potato Pits, 1878.

Vincent Van Gogh (1853-1890):
Peasant Woman, Brabant Headdress, 1885.

unpredicted by the costume studies of Italian peasants or the idealized peasant portraits of Robert.

Although the peasant was allowed the fragile individuality of the portrait, he was more often relegated to contrived genre scenes and shown against the background of his material life. If bourgeois portraits of the period gloried in details of chairs, mirrors, flowers, bibelots, and fireplaces, peasant genre painting was equally concerned with proper details of setting. It was necessary for peasant settings to be at once rugged and well maintained, and most pictures of peasant life stress an intimate harmony between the figures and their humble surroundings. Many examples could be cited. It is perhaps best to look at two rather late realist paintings of peasant genre, one from Scotland and the other by a German painter in Holland. W. D. McKay's *Field Working in Spring* of 1878 and Max Liebermann's *Village Street in Holland* of 1885 each represent a group of figures in a

Max Liebermann (1847-1935):
Village Street in Holland, 1885.

precisely observed context with tools, animals, wagons, and costumes. Both are specific to region, season, and task, and each particularizes with as much fervour as Robert or Schnetz generalized. Both are full of detailed observations, some of which help in the decoding of the image and some of which record distinctive features for their own sake. What these two pictures demonstrate is that truth of observation had become a more important part of European pictorial aesthetics by the late nineteenth century than either the quoting of other works of art or the creation of a coherent symbolic system within the picture. The strong natural connection between the peasantry and their environment was in itself the unifying intellectual force of the realist painting.

There is one troublesome notion which is central to the realist image of the peasant, and that is ugliness. When Max Liebermann exhibited his *Women Plucking Geese* in 1873, the popular press rose against it with the cry that Liebermann's figures, engaged in their oddly violent task, were distorted and disgusting. For these literate viewers, his peasant women were more ugly than real, and the picture was caricatured in the press, just as Manet's *Déjeuner sur l'Herbe* had been. This reading of the realist peasant must be seen as a counter to the notion of the beautiful or idealized peasant central to the classical tradition, and the very fact that the two attitudes were so different forces one to realize that each was somewhat false. Millet's peasants were condemned by no less a critic than Thoré for their ugliness, and the charge was levelled by many critics against other artists. The realist peasant emerges from these discussions as an ugly individual, scarred by work and worn by worry. Breton would never have allowed such wilful ugliness in his peasant paintings, yet it was for their prettiness that *he* was criticized by his realist contemporaries. We must remember that Liebermann's goosepluck-ing peasants, and many like them, were anti-idealist as much as they were realist.

Max Liebermann (1847-1935):
Women Plucking Geese, 1871-1872.

BEYOND REALISM:

The Peasant Image, 1880-1900

Adrien Lavieille (1818-1862):
Woodcut of 1853 after Millet's drawing
The Sheepshearers.

Vincent Van Gogh (1853-1890):
The Sheepshearers (after Millet), 1889.

In 1889 Vincent Van Gogh painted a series of small-scale peasant figures based on prints from earlier paintings by Millet. The affinity between the two artists has often been noted; each was concerned with the creation of a kind of painting which touched on the fundamentals of human existence and each was, to a large extent, a fatalist. Van Gogh, like Millet, had come into his own as a painter of rural life and his first masterpiece, *The Potato Eaters*, is one of the principal peasant paintings of the nineteenth century. Yet it would never have occurred to the mature Millet to make painted copies of another artist's works. He preferred to rely on his own experience, creating powerfully symbolic images based on his visual memories and ruminations on the peasant life around him. Van Gogh, on the other hand, anxious always to promote the power of the artist as an interpreter and transformer of reality, made his copies partly in homage to Millet, but partly also to endow the earlier artist's images with a greater conviction and force.

Indeed, Van Gogh revelled in his powers to transform. Where Millet's picture of the sheepshearers is quiet and serene, a study of interlocking masses and gently modulated hues, Van Gogh wrenched every ounce of life from his composition, denying any facial expression or individuality to the figures and enlivening the contours and colour areas with choppy, rapidly executed strokes of paint. Although he probably never knew the palette of the Millet painting

which he copied, he simplified and brightened it, making the female sheepshearer stand out in brilliant blue from the unified yellows, golden browns, and pale greens of her environment. Van Gogh all but ignored Millet's intricately conceived composition and chose instead to isolate the single working figure from the "ground" of her work. In this way she becomes an emblem of work, one of a series of such emblems derived from various compositions by Millet. The *Sheepshearers* and its companions (see page 84) reveal that, unlike the realists, Van Gogh believed fervently that great art sprang not from a faithful, or seemingly faithful, adherence to visual reality, but from the artist's transformation of that reality to suit his own specific ends.

It would be a mistake, of course, to deny this power of aesthetic transformation to the realists. Even our brief analysis of realist images of peasants has made it clear that their powers of selection and arrangement were considerable and that the aim of their art was to convey what one might call the appearance of reality. But Van Gogh, and many other artists of the last quarter of the nineteenth century, struggled to free their art from the grip of mimesis, the imitation of

nature, and it is perhaps curious that the peasant, who had been regarded throughout the century as the most natural of men, should play such an important role in the iconography of the most artificial or aestheticized of nineteenth-century styles, symbolism and the varieties of post-Impressionism.

But this late nineteenth-century anti-realism was not unprecedented. There was a strand of allegorical pastoralism in English painting of rural life in the early and mid nineteenth century, a strand linked intimately with English lyric poetry. The most important artist of this persuasion was Samuel Palmer, whose water-colours and drawings depict idyllic landscapes, most often with crops and peasant figures at moments of fullness and beauty. The *Harvest Moon* of 1831-1832 represents a peasant-filled landscape which is at once pastoral and agricultural. The immense moon illuminates this landscape and lends a symbolic aura to a decidedly imaginary nature. Palmer was uninterested in peasant costumes, in the details of props and poses, in the precise observation of natural forms, and his dismissal of realism must be seen in opposition to the descriptively literal

Thomas Armstrong (1835-1911):
The Hay Field, 1869.

world of most English watercolourists of the nineteenth century.

A similarly silent, dream-filled realm was painted in 1869 by the minor painter Thomas Armstrong. Using figural types and pictorial devices already explored by more expressly symbolist artists like Burne-Jones, Armstrong depicted what he called *The Hay Field*, a tightly contained and neatly manicured field in front of a farmhouse wall, all of which is presided over by three women and a sleeping child under the light of the moon. The women's clothing bears no relation to any known peasant costume, and their languid poses make it clear that their work is never to be performed in earnest. The very fact that this peasant image was made both after and undoubtedly with the knowledge of the peasant paintings of Millet, Courbet, and Breton, and

Camille Pissarro (1830-1903):
The Shepherdess (Peasant Girl with a Stick), 1881.

that it was contemporary with the realist images of McKay or Cameron in Great Britain, vouches for an anti-realism as deliberate as that of Palmer's watercolour. Each artist departed from the reality of rural life in England or any other country and used peasants as human props within pictures intended to evoke a pastoral mood. However, the centre of anti-realist pastoral and critical rhetoric was not England, but France in the 1880s. After more than thirty years of domination by realism, and its offshoots naturalism and Impressionism, French painters were weary of what some considered the crass materialism of modern art and began to develop the idea that pictures are artificial constructions governed by pictorial laws, and not transcriptions of material reality.

The artist who struggled probably more than any other to create a powerful painting rooted in observation, but beyond realism, was Camille Pissarro. His paintings of peasants underwent a slow but steady transformation away from descriptive realism in the 1880s. A canvas like *The Shepherdess* of 1881 is still a realist peasant image. Although the girl is not working at a definite task, but tending an unseen group of sheep or cattle, due attention is paid to facial features and working costume. The painting is far from being exact in its description, but it veers towards portraiture in ways consistent with the realist aesthetic. This young peasant girl is not a type, but an individual.

Pissarro's peasant images of the first half of the 1880s became increasingly complex and artificial in their grouping of figures and accessories, but the adherence to visual reality can always be felt. It was not until the middle of the decade that a change occurred, exemplified in *Apple Picking at Eragny* of 1888. The peasants seem almost to be dancing slowly in a landscape so insistently ordered and so responsive to their movements and gestures that it can hardly have been observed. There is an almost frozen airlessness to the picture, not the momentariness of realism, of a scene observed at a definite time. In many ways, Pissarro's *Apple Picking* is as artificially constructed as Léopold

Camille Pissarro (1830-1903):
Apple Picking at Eragny, 1888.

Robert's *Madonna dell'Arco*, although this artifice is not motivated by an interest in ideal beauty based on antique and Renaissance art.

What, one must ask, was the nature of Pissarro's transformation of the peasantry? How and to what end did he create a synthesized peasant image? The affinities with Millet's peasant world are superficially great, but after a closer look it becomes clear that Pissarro departed from Millet's example as insistently as did Van Gogh. Millet's peasants are always involved in a relentless seasonal cycle of work which subjugated their beings, and their bodies, to the ravages of nature in time. Pissarro's peasants work more easily, in collective groupings in which their efforts are minimized and the strain of their labour rarely, if ever, felt. The bounty of Millet's earth is meagre; that of Pissarro, although basic, is considerable. It is clear that Pissarro was not an Old Testament fatalist, as was his great predecessor, in the crowded field of peasant genre painters. Indeed, there is a mood of optimism in Pissarro's peasant world. This world remains as a pictorial expression of Pissarro's belief that "work is the moral regulator of man" and that through work,

collective work, man can gain a humanized control of his natural environment. For Millet, man is controlled by the rhythm of the seasons; for Pissarro, the seasons are used by man as the basis for a productive agriculture. Pissarro's peasant images have their iconological sources not in the peasant novel, travel literature, or lyric poetry, but in the socio-political writings of men like Proudhon, Kropotkin, Grave and Reclus. The anarchist concept of an agro-industrial state in which all men would give some of their labours to agriculture was endorsed by Pissarro, and his peasant images must be seen almost as pictorial advertisements for the joys of agricultural work. It was, indeed, Pissarro's surrendering of the peasant image to these socio-political ideals which forced him to abandon peasant realism. The life of peasants was not in itself an ideal. Rather, it was to be part of a new ideal society for which Pissarro anxiously sought pictorial equivalents.

If Pissarro was to transform real peasants into ideal agro-industrial workers using political theory as a basis for his pictorial decisions, Gauguin and his followers in Brittany had no such ideological motive for their antirealist

Paul Gauguin (1848-1903):
La Belle Angèle, 1889.

peasant images of the late 1880s and early 1890s. Unlike Pissarro, but like many painters of the peasantry, Gauguin was fascinated by peasant devotion, particularly by its almost pagan manifestations in rural Brittany. But, whereas artists from Boudin to Dagnan-Bouveret painted carefully composed realist canvases of the pardons of Brittany, Gauguin transformed the peasant religious experience into images which use self-consciously primitive pictorial devices and become, as a result, utterly unpicturesque. Gauguin contorted peasant physiognomies so that his figures function neither as individuals nor as standard peasant types in the sense of Millet's generalized peasants. Most of his paintings make it clear that he avoided the "beautiful," and even *La Belle Angèle*, an allegorical peasant portrait, raises unsettling questions about vanity and religion by the abrupt juxtaposition of Christian and seemingly pagan forms and of "real" and "imaginary" pictorial areas. The costumed peasant woman is completely bovine and occupies, with all her placid righteousness, a circular area which seems to be neither a picture nor a mirror. She becomes an object at once of adoration and contempt. Her principal characteristic is her religious and sexual ambiguity. She is neither beautiful nor even meaningful, but disturbingly unreal. For Gauguin, in *La Belle Angèle*, the peasant becomes an abstraction of the peasant image.

Gauguin's followers, Sérusier and Bernard, each painted many peasant pictures and, although they are closer in their composition and subjects to standardized peasant genre types, they infuse those types with the same disturbing unreality as Gauguin's peasant paintings. Sérusier's *Solitude* of 1890–1892 is virtually a remaking of Pissarro's *Shepherdess* of ten years earlier. Yet, where Pissarro's peasant is modestly engaging and charming, Sérusier's is ill-proportioned, ugly, thwarting. In her rugged features she seems to partake of her rocky setting, and her heavy-lidded, suspicious glare tells the viewer that her solitude has been disturbed.

Emile Bernard (1868-1941):
Breton Women on a Wall, 1892.

Paul Sérusier (1864-1927):
Solitude, 1890-1892.

Bernard too, in a series of Breton peasant paintings made in 1890–1892, created artificial groupings of costumed peasant figures both at work and at rest which everywhere elude the viewer. In *Breton Women on a Wall* the costumes, bodies, gestures, and positions of the figures are contorted in such a way as to produce a painting in which there is no internal unity of mood or activity. For Bernard, as for Gauguin and Sérusier, the world of the Breton peasant was a closed world, inaccessible in its primitiveness to the modern viewer. They each painted peasants who existed without the clear purpose of the peasants described by Robert, Millet, Breton, even Pissarro. The cultural distance between the artist and his humble yet mysterious subjects is celebrated in brilliant colour areas awkwardly bounded by lines.

It is important to remember that many realist paintings of Breton peasants were made both before and after the difficult canvases by Gauguin and his followers. Indeed, because of its regional distinctiveness and the tradition of tourism following Chateaubriand's *Mémoires d'outre-tombe* of 1849, Brittany and its rural populace were pictured countless times by European and American artists in search of picturesque subjects. Gauguin's paintings look the way they do not because of Brittany, but because their maker was attempting to create a new and more powerful peasant painting than either the classical painters of the 1820s and

Jean-Charles Cazin (1841-1901):
The Day's Work Done, 1889.

1830s or the realists of the middle and later nineteenth century. To do so, he devised an "artificial" style deriving from widely divergent sources, some of them outside the European tradition. He also strove to paint peasant subjects which were either unprecedented or so ambiguously related to precedent that precise comparison becomes impossible. Even if one could accept the peasant as a symbol for all mankind, or for mankind at its most basic level, Gauguin's peasant images set that archetype at so distant a remove from the modern viewer that clear understanding is difficult. Indeed, it is easier to compare Gauguin's peasant images with nineteenth-century accounts of peasants as savages whose culture was seen as the first stage in the process of evolution from barbarism to civilization. As the historian of the French peasantry, Eugen Weber, has put it, "From Balzac to Zola, through Maeterlinck, the Abbé Roux, and many others, the peasant appears as a dark, mysterious, hostile, and menacing figure and is described as such. Where he is not a noble savage, as he was for George Sand, he is simply a savage." Gauguin, like Pissarro, despised the urban civilization of modern France. Yet his images of French peasants do not portray a rosy, "natural" alternative to the corruption of Paris. Indeed, Gauguin, like Bernard and Sérusier, became a kind of pictorial anthropologist, obsessed not by his peasant subjects themselves, but by their distance from him.

Before discussing several other anti-realist developments of the late nineteenth century, it is necessary to stress the fact that, of the great anti-realist painters of the peasantry, none was reared as a peasant or in close touch with rural civilization. By contrast, every great realist painter of the peasantry, at least in France, was familiar with them from childhood and felt at home living and painting in a rural milieu. This was emphatically not the case with Pissarro, Gauguin, Sérusier, Bernard, or even Van Gogh. Pissarro was born in the West Indies to a prosperous family of merchants. Gauguin, Sérusier, and Bernard were all from wealthy bourgeois families and, like Pissarro, grew up in urban, mercantile surroundings. None of them possessed what one might call the birthright to be a sympathetic portrayer of peasant life, as did Millet, Courbet, Breton, Bastien-Lepage, or Lhermitte. As a result of this sociological distance from their subject, the anti-realist painters were unable or unwilling to portray peasant life fully. Pissarro avoided religious festivals, costumes, and other ethnographically interesting aspects of the French peasant culture he painted. Conversely, Gauguin's peasant realm has practically no images of the labour of the fields, and Van Gogh's rules out both commerce and conviviality. These selective portrayals reveal clearly that the peasant himself was not an engrossing object of interest for the anti-realists. Their pictorial world includes as many images that have no connection with the peasantry as those that do. Again, the contrast with the major realist painters of the peasantry—except Courbet—can be made very starkly. When Millet, Breton, or Lhermitte chose to paint peasant life, their choice was whole-hearted and their lives thenceforth were committed to a pictorial record of rural civilization. For the anti-realist painters of the peasantry, the

modern artist was responsible for a much wider range of subjects. The peasant had ceased to be an acceptable metaphor for all of man.

One major French artist who made many anti-realist paintings of peasants is largely forgotten. Collected throughout the world during his lifetime, the paintings of Jean-Charles Cazin are most often found today in the museum store-rooms of France and the United States, and there has not been a Cazin exhibition for over two generations. He specialized in wistful, poetic landscapes and allegorical peasant compositions which somehow straddled the worlds of Corot and Puvis de Chavannes. *The Day's Work Done* of 1889 represents a peasant couple with their child standing together in the vastness of a bleak landscape in northern France. The pictorial analogies with the holy family are numerous and the composition is so obviously contrived that one hardly accepts the painting as realist. Rather, it evokes a mood of religious reverie and gentle melancholy far from the rigours of real peasant life in so desolate a place. Many of Cazin's most beautiful figure paintings of the 1880s and 1890s transpose scenes from

Jean-Charles Cazin (1841-1901):
Flight into Egypt.

the Bible or classical literature into humble peasant settings in France. In this way they aim at a timelessness which is both literary and pictorial. When compared with the revolutionary intentions of Pissarro or the despairing modernism of Gauguin and his followers, Cazin can be considered reactionary and conservative. His work has its roots in Corot and the world of the classical peasant. It looks not to the future, but to the past.

Perhaps the greatest painter of the peasantry in the last quarter of the nineteenth century outside France was the North Italian, Giovanni Segantini. Like Van Gogh, he based his early style on that of Millet and began to paint independently important works in the early 1880s. His first great masterpiece, *Ave Maria on the Water*, was painted in 1886 and is now housed in a museum devoted to his work in St. Gall, Switzerland. It can be described absolutely as symbolist. Its subject, a peasant mother and child with their flock of lambs and sheep crossing a lake in a simple boat, is so filled with allusions to regeneration through religion that it was clearly "conceived" rather than observed. Again, as was the case with Cazin, Segantini infused peasant reality with symbolic ideas, and not unlike Cazin, his peasant world was optimistic in its mystical pantheism. The accord between the peasant, his tasks, his animals, and his environment is underscored by compositional and chromatic devices which stress unity. The harmonic rhythm of peasant figures and animals in light is the subject of many paintings by Segantini, and they paved the way for the later achievements of Italian peasants like Morbelli and Pellizza. Although, like Pissarro, these latter artists put their art to the service of political ideology, their methods of pictorial construction were close to those of Segantini who conceived of the peasant as the harmonious ideal for all human life. This essentially regressive ideology was shared by many artists outside France who, using the peasant as a figure in complete accord with his setting, created a new and self-consciously decorative peasant genre painting.

Giovanni Segantini (1858-1899): *Ave Maria on the Water,* 1886.

II

THE MEANINGS
OF THE
PEASANT IMAGE

Sir Edwin Landseer (1802-1873):
A Highland Breakfast, 1834.

BETWEEN NATURE AND CULTURE:
The Peasant and Civilization

It is fair to say that the nineteenth century was a period dominated by dichotomies. Whether Hegelian or Baudelairian, the conceptual systems of philosophy, the arts, and even history tended to state their case in terms of "either/or," and the image of the peasant was no exception. Mass migrations and class mobility created a situation in much of Europe in which men and women of peasant origin began increasingly to break into the world of intellectuals, industrialists, and politicians. This very fact forced Europeans into a direct confrontation with peasant culture, and predictably their ranks split into two groups. The first conceived of the peasant as little more than an animal, as man without culture. The second, imbued with nationalist trends, saw peasant culture as real culture or culture at the base of national civilization, free from the artifice of urban life. The first of these readings of the peasant has a distinguished expression in literature, but not in the visual arts. The second found equal expression in both.

La Bête Humaine: The Peasant as Animal

"Of all useful animals, woman is the one that the Roman peasant uses most profitably." So Edmond About began his discussion of Roman peasant women in his *Rome Contemporaine* of 1861. For him the peasant woman was quite simply an animal, and a most useful one, and this idea, startling at first, was developed further by him in an analysis of her life of never-ending toil. About was by no means alone in considering the peasant, whether male or female, to be an animal, and if Georges Lecomte called peasants "le végétal humain" in one sentence, he transformed them equally into "la bête humaine" in another. Even popular proverbs embodied this notion: in France, "Jacques Bonhomme has a strong back and will bear anything"; in Germany, "A peasant is just like an ox, only he has no horns." The peasant was treated as an animal, a human beast, in so many novels, travel accounts, and memoirs that to quote samples hardly gives an idea of the prevalence of the metaphor. Stendhal called the Italian peasants of Piacenza bestial and vicious,

sophisticated only in their ferocity and vengeance, and in this way Stendhal's image of the peasant transcends that of the "useful animals" and enters a realm of terrifying wildness. Taine was only slightly more sympathetic, likening the sheepskin-clad peasant children he had seen to a troop of wild colts. These notions were applied equally to French, Spanish, and Italian peasants, particularly those who lived in wild, desolate landscapes far from the civilizing influences of manor houses, churches, and towns.

In another twist of this animal metaphor for the peasantry, writers were obsessed and disgusted by the extent to which peasants lived among animals. The English writer and painter Edward Lear, travelling in Italy in the 1840s, expressed horror at peasant living conditions in a way typical of many similar texts: "The habitation was so dirty and wretched... while I was sitting near the chimney (it had the additional charm of being a smoking one), I was startled by the entrance of several large pigs who passed very much at their ease through the kitchen."

There are several notable representations of animals in peasant living quarters, and Landseer's sentimental *Highland Breakfast* of 1834 was one of the earliest and most admired of them. It was exhibited at the Royal Academy in the year it was painted and sent to the Exposition Universelle of 1855 in Paris, where its frank comparative juxtaposition of canine and human life was noted by the realist critic Théophile Gautier. For all the charm and apparent naïveté of Landseer's painting, it raised disturbing questions about the relationship between human and animal life, questions which were left to be explored more fervently in literature than in the pictorial arts. Perhaps the most famous novel which revels in these animalist techniques is Zola's *La Terre* of 1887, which begins with a young woman taking her cow to be impregnated by a bull and meeting her eventual lover while they witness the mating. Later in the novel, Zola juxtaposes the birth of a child with the birth of a calf. A similar juxtaposition is made by the Polish peasant novelist Ladislas Reymont in his short story entitled *The Bitch* published in 1897. He contrasts a "beast-like" woman who tortures her child with a "humane" dog who saves her puppies. Writers of rural genre excelled in drawing parallels between natural and human life, and the gist of their observations is that all human beings, and particularly peasants, are animals.

There are also popular images which deal forthrightly with the close rapport between peasants and their animals. François Grenier, in a lithograph of 1851 entitled *They Understand Each Other*, depicts an old peasant woman in the fields with her goats and, unlike those in Liebermann's *Woman with Goats in the Dunes* (see page 88), this old woman's goats understand her perfectly. The natural communication between animal and peasant is the subject of many barnyard and pasture scenes in which peasants talk to their animals in an everyday fashion or simply stand together with them as if in an almost mystical accord. It was Millet's picture of the *Newborn Calf* which drew, perhaps, the most severe criticism for expressing this sympathetic understanding, bordering on reverence, of human beings for their animals.

The almost cretinous peasants in the picture solemnly carry a calf born in the fields back to their farmyard. There is an implicit reference to the biblical golden calf; the animal is to be worshipped, and the peasant men become beasts of burden.

Certain painters extended the metaphor of the peasant-as-animal into their depictions of peasants themselves. Millet was accused, unjustly, both by Breton and Thoré, of making his peasants ugly and bestial, of depriving them of humanity by his contorting of their features to express their blind submission to fate. Many writers of the twentieth century have found Gauguin's peasants either bestial or bovine, and painters in other countries were accused of making their peasants hideous and too much like animals.

What is remarkable, however, is the small extent to which a prevalent literary metaphor, the peasant-as-animal, was expressed in the pictorial arts. Even the many illustrations made for various editions of Zola's *La Terre* contain few instances in which the animalism of the text is reinforced by the illustrations, and paintings of peasants tend, almost by definition, to humanize and ennoble their subjects, to treat them as part of human society and as part of a new humanized art of the modern world.

◁ François Grenier de Saint-Martin (1793-1867):
They Understand Each Other, 1851. Lithograph.

Jean-François Millet (1814-1875):
Bringing Home the Newborn Calf, 1864.

Custom and Costume: The Peasant, Ethnography, and Folklore

Equally strong as the image of the peasant-as-animal, especially during the latter half of the nineteenth century with the development of the disciplines of social anthropology and folklore, was the image of the peasant as a man with his own customs and traditions, all of which were different from those of "civilized" urban man, but which comprised his culture nevertheless. Although social anthropology was responsible for this more generalized definition of culture, distinct from "being civilized," most social anthropologists devoted their energies to theoretical speculations made from the comfort of their library armchairs. The true study of the culture of the inhabitants of rural Europe was left to the newly formed field of folklore. The original German term *Volkskunde* was a word created around 1806 in Germany with the publication of a collection of folksongs by Clemens Brentano and Achim von Arnim. Indeed, not until W. J. Thoms first used the word folklore in English in 1846 did non-German Europeans undertake in earnest the regional ethnographic studies which had been part of German academic research since the beginning of the century. The discipline of folklore, like its sister discipline of social anthropology, was rooted in nineteenth-century evolutionary theory, particularly the concept of

unilineal evolution popular at the time. Peasants were viewed as the primitive people of European society, and their religion and superstitions, stories and songs, artefacts and tools, as survivals or relics from a previous stage of social evolution. With all the preconceptions of romanticism, the folklorists believed that, by recording the customs of the rural peoples of Europe, they were recording their own past. For this reason, they stimulated an avid interest in regional cultures and popular traditions throughout western and eastern Europe and by the later decades of the nineteenth century it had become fashionable in the evening salons of the urban haute bourgeoisie to recount peasant folk tales.

While folklorists recorded in writing the oral and material traditions of the peasantry, and composers from Beethoven to Bartok and Janacek incorporated peasant songs in their music, painters and printmakers were the visual ethnographers, devoting themselves particularly to the accurate depiction of folk costume. Illustrated albums of peasant types in all their regional finery were among the most cherished and expensive books to be found in middle-class and aristocratic homes. Examples of such albums are numerous. In his *Sketches of the*

Bartolomeo Pinelli (1781-1835):
(1) *Peasant Family of the Roman Campagna.*
(2) *Hay Wagons driven from the Campagna into Rome on the way to the Barns in June.*
(3) *At the Door of a Country Inn.*
Prints, 1820.

Franz Catel (1778-1856):
Italian Shepherds, c. 1820-1825.

Country, Character, and Costume, in Portugal and Spain, published in 1809, William Bradford presents us with a series of pictures of somewhat stiff but colourful peasant figures wearing their local dress. In 1820 the Italian engraver Bartolomeo Pinelli, who specialized in recording the customs and habits of his native country, published a more sophisticated and pictorially complex inventory of diverse costumes, placing his groups of peasant figures in country settings. Some allusion is made to occupation, to their identity as rural labourers, though clearly as an afterthought to the attention given to their attire. The similarities between Pinelli's prints and paintings by Robert and other foreign painters in Italy during the first half of the nineteenth century are evident. The German painter Franz Catel, in his *Italian Shepherds* of the early 1820s, carefully posed a young peasant girl in her regional costume and a shepherd in his typical attire against an unimposing backdrop. All our interest is focused upon the richly coloured clothing worn by these anonymous Italian peasant types. In another picture, *Italian Popular Life near Pozzuoli*, Catel, who became known as a student of the popular culture of southern Italy, placed his costumed figures in an ethnographic-ally interesting context and showed them

Franz Catel (1778-1856):
*Scene of Italian Popular Life
near Pozzuoli*, c. 1823.

François Charpentier:
*Peasant Couple in the Landes Travelling
on Stilts*, c. 1830. Lithograph.

Landais en voyage.

Lith. de Charpentier.

dancing the lively tarantella which was as much a part of Neapolitan culture as the can-can was to become of Parisian culture. The French painter Montessuy, in his *Peasant Festival at Cerbara* of 1847, used this costumed dancing theme again. Both pictures are visual ethnographic records not only of regional dress but also of popular forms of celebration; they relate closely to a tradition established by Léopold Robert in the *Madonna dell'Arco* where a study of costumes is associated with a popular festival which was clearly important to the rural folk of the region. Similar pictures were made by German and Swiss artists working at home, such as Wolfgang Adam Toepffer and Ludwig Knaus. While Montessuy's joyous portrait of peasant life may appear exaggerated, it was not in fact ethnographically inaccurate. Hippolyte Taine, during his journey to Italy in the 1860s,

Jean-François Montessuy (1804-1876):
Peasant Festival at Cerbara, 1847.

François Charpentier:
Two Peasant Women in the Neighbourhood of Rouen,
c. 1830. Lithograph.

mentions seeing a cartload of singing peasants, and numerous other travellers wrote lengthy descriptions of regional festivals.

The composition of Catel's simpler figure painting *Italian Shepherds* is equally characteristic of the work of perhaps the greatest of French printmakers contributing to the costume book genre, the lithographer François Charpentier. His prints are accompanied by specific locative titles, and the attention to clothing, and especially headdress, is minute in its detail. Rarely are there more than two figures placed together, and rarely is any reference made to work or occupation. If these are rural folk, and often we can only identify them as such by Charpentier's use of the words *paysans* or *paysannes*, then they are rural folk wearing their Sunday best, their most picturesque and typical regional costume. Indeed, one English traveller

François Charpentier:
*Peasant Couple of Saint-Théogonec
in the Finistère*, c. 1830. Lithograph.

to Italy in the 1860s worried about the contradiction between the supposedly "dirty" work of the peasant and his impeccable attire, and another distinguished between the "former" and "present" costumes of the women of Scanno in Italy. Although this latter traveller fails to offer us any insight as to why there was a transformation, the distinction he makes is important. The French historian Emmanuel Le Roy Ladurie has demonstrated that, far from being ancient and rooted in the peasant past, many of the peasant costumes recorded in nineteenth-century prints and paintings were of recent origin. They are elaborations which developed not only as a result of the economic and demographic expansion of the countryside, but also of the growing interest in folklore and

Paul Gauguin (1848-1903):
Four Breton Women, 1886.

Maurice Denis (1870-1943):
Peasant Woman with Cow, 1893.

Jens Ferdinand Willumsen (1863-1958):
Breton Women Walking, 1890.

regional culture, indeed, to a certain extent, as part of an interest in creating a picturesque past for these ''noble savages,'' thought to be the ancestors of the urban bourgeoisie who bought and delighted in the printed and painted costume studies.

In France during the later decades of the nineteenth century it was the costumes and customs of the people of Brittany in particular which captured the imagination of folklorists and artists alike. Breton culture was thought to have remained more intact than that of any other province. Commenting on this region, the leading French travel-guide writer of the nineteenth century, Adolphe Joanne, wrote: ''Brittany offers a character more distinct, more startling, more original... her more poetic traditions... the population is distinguished from that of other provinces by its physical features, its costumes, its habits, its customs, beliefs, superstitions; in a word, Brittany is one of the true curiosities of France.'' Joanne says little more in his guide about the people and traditions, and it is to the folklorists and artists of the later nineteenth century that we must turn for a fuller account of the costumes and superstitions, legends and songs of the Breton peasant.

Paul Gauguin, Emile Bernard, Maurice Denis, and other artists both French and foreign painted many pictures of Breton peasants. Perhaps the most accurate are those of an artist now little known, Pascal Adolphe Dagnan-Bouveret. He paid close attention to the rendering of Breton peasant costumes and, as in the lithographs of Charpentier, to the Breton headdresses in particular. These starched white caps seemed to symbolize, more than anything

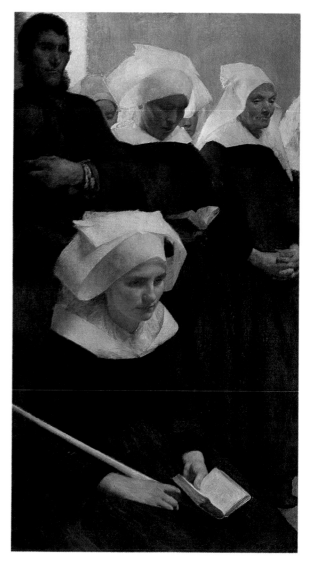

P. A. J. Dagnan-Bouveret (1852-1929):
Pardon in Brittany, 1888.

Paul Gauguin (1848-1903):
The Yellow Christ, 1889.

else, the cultural purity and religious spirit which came to be identified with this population of western France, a population surviving in an increasingly modern and anticlerical world. Dagnan-Bouveret's pictures are at one and the same time costume studies and studies of folk religion, that is, religion in an ethnographic sense rather than in the moralistic or idealistic sense associated with pictures like Millet's *Angelus*. His pardons of Brittany depict religious festivals which had been celebrated by the local peasants for several hundred years. The cos-

Eugène Boudin (1824-1898):
The Pardon of Sainte-Anne-La-Palud, 1858.

P. A. J. Dagnan-Bouveret (1852-1929):
Breton Women at a Pardon, 1887.

tumes in them are in fact festival costumes, worn only at these times and perhaps at other important life-cycle events such as marriages, and the expert ethnographer or folklorist would probably be able to identify the home parish of these female peasant figures by their headdress. The challenge to the ethnographer-folklorist would be even greater in Boudin's expansive rendering of the *Pardon of Sainte-Anne-La-Palud*, where a variety of both costumes and activities are evident. It is worth noting, if only to do justice to Dagnan-Bouveret, the difference in both style and sentiment between these two pardon images. As the critic Paul Mantz observed, Dagnan-Bouveret's pictures possess a kind of archaic simplicity which links his Breton peasants more to the past than the present. A similar archaism informs Gauguin's *Yellow Christ* of 1889, which unites fundamentally institutional religion with folk religion in its depiction of three peasant women bowed in prayer at the foot of a wooden crucifix set in a Breton landscape.

While Brittany provided the major regional subject matter for the better known painter-ethnographers of peasant life, other regions of France were depicted by lesser known artists who gave equal attention to regional folk costumes and folk customs. Gustave Brion painted pictures of Alsatian weddings and festivals; Emile Loubon portrayed the peasants of the Béarn; and Philippe Jeanron, in a rather early picture dated 1834, painted the costumed peasants of the Limousin. Elsewhere in Europe, a similar regional pictorial tradition was underway. The art historian Richard Muther has described the paintings of Adolph Tidemand in

Adolph Tidemand (1814-1876):
Norwegian Country Girl as a Bride, 1849.

Philippe Jeanron (1807-1877):
Peasants of the Limousin, 1834.

Ernest Biéler (1863-1948):
Swiss Women Plaiting Straw, c. 1900.

Hugo Salmson (1844-1894):
At the Gate of Dalby (Skåne), Sweden, 1884.

Anders Zorn (1860-1920):
*Midsummer Dance
in a Swedish Village,* 1897.

Norway as an "ethnographical course of instruction in the life of a distant race as yet unknown in the rest of Europe." His picture of a rural bride captures the costumed richness of this important event in the life of a young peasant girl. In Switzerland the early work of Ernest Biéler comes close to Tidemand in its wealth of costume detail. The Czech painter Josef Mánes collected folktales and folksongs in addition to images as he travelled through his native land. In Sweden, Anders Zorn, in later life, returned to his native Mora and decided to spend part of each year painting peasants in their regional dress. His compatriot Hugo Salmson did likewise, after spending several years painting the French peasants of Picardy. By the end of the nineteenth century, in 1886 to be exact, an anonymous writer in the recently founded *Revue des Traditions Populaires* commented on "Le Folklore au Salon" and expressed disappointment at the meagre showing for that year: "Few indeed are the painters who have drawn their inspiration from the sources of popular tradition." It was as if painters had come to be expected to depict rural life with ethnographic accuracy.

François-André Vincent (1746-1816):
Agriculture, 1798.

THE PEASANT IMAGE
AND BOURGEOIS VALUES

Among its history paintings, historical landscapes, battle scenes, portraits, and still lifes, the Paris Salon of 1798 contained a picture entitled *Agriculture* by François-André Vincent. The descriptive entry in the Salon catalogue is worth quoting: "Convinced of the fact that agriculture is the basis of the prosperity of nations, the painter has represented a father accompanied by his wife and daughter visiting a ploughman at work. He shows his respect by looking on during the lesson which he has asked the ploughman to give his son, whose education he would regard as imperfect without this knowledge."

For Vincent and the bourgeois patron for this and other paintings (the textile manufacturer from Toulouse, François-Bernard Boyer-Fonfrède), the work of the fields was a noble work and the peasant worker an honest and commendable citizen of the State. Vincent's peasant ploughman was given the head and muscular body of a High Renaissance figure and his hand, pointing in instruction to the great pair of oxen, is quoted directly from an engraved reproduction of the hand of God in Michelangelo's *Creation of Adam* on the Sistine ceiling. It has been pointed out, with justice, that in painting this picture Vincent was representing a scene from rural life as an *exemplum virtutis*, and that the intellectual precedent for this comes almost directly from the moral philosophy of the enlightenment as expressed by J. J. Rousseau. With this superb picture, peasant life became a subject for the moral reflection of the modern urban man, and by the middle of the century peasant images were so common in the Salon that no explanatory texts like that quoted above were needed. Indeed, pictures of strong peasant ploughmen after Vincent had no need of a bourgeois family to make them *exempla virtutis*. With this painting Vincent had begun a tradition of the representation of rural or peasant life which was to be a principal pictorial preoccupation of the nineteenth century and which was clearly made for an urban bourgeois audience.

In the absence of a careful study of the patronage of peasant paintings, it is difficult to make accurate statements about the ideological basis of the peasant image. Yet, using common sense and historical evidence, it becomes apparent that, in a good many cases, pictures of peasants were used as carriers of the cultural values of the bourgeoisie. Historians of the rise of the French bourgeoisie after the Revolution of 1789 have stressed the importance of certain bourgeois values used to guide and maintain class superiority. Many of these, particularly those involving domestic real estate and education, were incapable of being pictured, especially using peasants as carriers. However, some of the fundamental values of bourgeois society—work, family, religion, and patriotism—were embodied time and time again in the peasant image. As a kind of Everyman, the peasant served to render absolute these values and further to suggest that they were generally human rather than bourgeois. While there is

LES TRAVAUX ET LES HABITANTS DU VILLAGE.

Petits! Petits! Petits!   *Femmes faisant des fromages.*   *Garde champêtre.*   *Laitière.*   *Jeannette trait les vaches.*

"The Labours and Inhabitants of the Village."
French popular print (Image d'Epinal), 1856.

considerable evidence to suggest that certain peasants were centrally concerned with family unity or were deeply religious, other evidence makes it clear that feelings of family unity among the peasantry varied with differences in inheritance systems and that rural religiousness was not everywhere on the rise in the nineteenth century. In fact, peasants, like their urban counterparts whether bourgeois or proletariat, had no unified system of values, and the fact that such a large percentage of peasant pictures embody one of the four values mentioned above is proof of the ideological importance of those pictures to their audience. The peasant image served to teach "real" values to the bourgeoisie, while the peasant himself was plagued by many of the same ills—unemployment, malaise, ambition, and alcoholism—as was the bourgeoisie.

This study is too brief for a full discussion of the subtleties and varieties of class ideology as embodied in peasant pictures. But the subject is not as complex as might be supposed. Indeed, no matter what conflicting values motivated either peasants or the bourgeoisie in reality, the pictures representing the one class for the other are often touchingly naïve and easy to interpret. They tend to be pictorial emblems for verbal messages which are no more or less sophisticated than "family unity is good" or "piety is good." The peasant carried these simple messages in a simple way, and it is perhaps not accidental that the paintings of Millet and Van Gogh are among the most popular in the world because of their powerful clarity and simplicity. Most modern city-dwellers have no idea whatsoever about peasants, but the peasant image continues to embody values they hold dear.

Work

Whatever their conflicting social attitudes towards the peasantry, writers who described it were united in their view that the peasant's life was, or should be, a life devoted to hard work. Travel writers, in their frequent exposition of the miseries or joys of the peasants they passed on their journeys to and from major cities throughout Europe, devoted countless passages to what one British writer called "the toilers of the field," and peasants were often admired as much for their physical strength as for their picturesque costumes or curious festivals. One visitor to Spain in the 1820s summarized the typical day of a Spanish peasant in this laconic phrase: "He rises early and after mass goes forth to labour." Even those observers who found the peasant "lazy" or "idle," or who described his living conditions as "abounding in filth," made these comments from the ideological position that it was the peasant's duty to work and that only by hard work could the miseries of his life be alleviated. For one eloquent moralist writing at mid-century, "peasants know, or act as if they know, that work is the regeneration of matter, the sanctification of thought, an active prayer which the industrious send up incessantly to the creator."

Painters interested in the peasantry had a more difficult time, at least initially, in their attempts to portray peasant work. The standard repertoire of poses and gestures learned by painters like Robert, Schnetz, Becker, or even Waldmüller was based either on antique sculpture or on certain newer positions derived from

J. Blondeau:
Agriculture, 1874. Lithograph.

their study of professional models in the studio. Neither of these sources for the study of the human figure was useful for the description of physical labour. The strain and muscle tension of work were at once too disfiguring to the body to be thought truly beautiful and occurred too rapidly to be carefully studied by the artist. Throughout the century these problems plagued artists interested in the accurate description of the working human form, with the result that paintings of work do not appear in profusion until the middle of the century and that many of them have a stilted, constructed quality. According to the English painter Walter Sickert, Millet "knew that if figures in movement were to be painted so as to be convincing, it must be a process of cumulative observation," and he contrasted such a process which, to him, occurred in Millet and Degas, with the process of working from static poses that ruined the paintings of artists like Bastien-Lepage who, to Sickert, simply "catalogued facts."

The earliest systematic attempts to describe peasant work were popular images based not on careful study of individual figures but on rapid sketches of clothed working figures made from nature. Perhaps the earliest "summa" of rural work was W. H. Pyne's *Microcosm*, the lengthy subtitle of which tells us all we need to know about it: "A Picturesque Delineation of the Arts, Agriculture, Manufactures, etc., of Great Britain. In a series of Above 600 Groups of Small Figures for the Embellishment of Landscape and Comprising the Most Interesting Subjects in Rural and Domestic Scenery, in External and Internal Navigation, in Country Sports and Employments, in the Arts of War and Peace. The Whole Accurately Drawn from Nature, and Etched by W. H. Pyne; and Aquatinted by J. Hill." First published in instalments, the collection was issued twice in complete form, in 1808 and 1824, and was perhaps the most influential book of its kind printed during the first half of the nineteenth century. Numerous later books illustrating the tasks of rural workers were produced in both Great Britain and France, and most of them owed a considerable debt to

Pyne's monumental visual encyclopaedia. In fact, many French popular images of peasant work made at a much later date are not essentially dissimilar. The two illustrated here date from the mid-1850s and the mid-1870s respectively, and they each represent on a single sheet a multitude of rural tasks being performed in miniature. None of these tasks is ennobled by enlargement or careful study, and the notion they convey is not very different from that of Pyne, that rural work is a continuous though varied set of activities most of which are concerned with the production of food. Such "microcosms" of rural life abounded throughout the nineteenth century, and even artists like Millet, Lhermitte, Bastien-Lepage, and Pissarro worked towards such compendia of miniature scenes of rural labour. Pissarro's version, *Les Travaux des Champs*, was a continuous preoccupation of the artist from 1886 until his death in 1903, when it was left unfinished, largely because neither Pissarro nor his son Lucien could decide whether the text should be politically or poetically motivated. Millet's earlier version, *Les Travaux des Champs*, as well as Bastien-Lepage's *Les Mois Rustiques* were also left incomplete. Perhaps only Lhermitte, of the peasant painters, was a successful purveyor of mass-produced images of peasant labour, and prints from his work appeared in widely circulated magazines as well as books.

Léon Lhermitte (1844-1925):
Ploughing, 1889. Wood engraving.

for hundreds of other texts. The great French historian Michelet, in his fervent book *Le Peuple*, rooted French society in the image of the peasant attending church after a hard week of work in the fields, and many theorists of private property thought that physical labour on the land constituted a right to ownership, and considered the landowning peasant to be the true foundation of society.

All these verbal and visual images which discuss peasant labour as a whole phenomenon make the important assumption that peasants produced food not only for themselves, but also for the nation. Yet this belief that the agricultural surplus of the peasant family would be food for all society can be considered now to be both optimistic and, in a sense, inaccurate. The contrary idea of the peasant as a merely self-sufficient rural labourer, scraping a bare subsistence from the soil, can also be found repeatedly in texts, factual and fictional, of the period. As Edmond About put it, peasants "spend their life earning their living. The existence of this class is like a vicious circle." About was certainly not the only observer to describe peasant life in isolated terms, yet, in view of this economically negative portrait, the popular printed images which portray the peasant as a productive labourer must be interpreted as ideologically modernist and progressive, rather than as decriptions of peasant life.

If we turn from these printed images to paintings of peasant life, the terrain becomes more complex and interpretation more problematic. Not only was the technical problem of depicting working figures enormously hampering to the painter, but also the many, often contradictory attitudes towards the meaning of physical work in an age of industrial modernism made it difficult for the painter to be precise about his intentions. There are, however, several general notions which are given repeated expression in paintings of rural labour. The first, and most pervasive, is that peasant work occurs in seasonal time and that it has a slow, natural rhythm unlike the modern, repetitive work of the urban labourer. Marcel Charlot, in his *Paysages*

The ideology of these images is simple. Each conceives of the peasant as "the nation's physical backbone and bulwark of its social order." "Their presence," as the same writer, William H. Dawson, put it as late as 1901, "is a national blessing." Dawson was an Englishman writing about Germany, but his remarks are so typical of nationalist writing about peasant life throughout northern Europe that they can stand

Fritz von Uhde (1848-1911):
The Gleaners, 1889.

Camille Pissarro (1830-1903):
Peasant Women Setting Props for Peas,
1890. Gouache.

Emile Bernard (1868-1941):
The Buckwheat Harvest, 1888.

et Paysans, published in 1898 and illustrated by Lhermitte, wrote extensively of the connection between natural time and religious experience and feared that the rise of industry would ruin the true life of the country by destroying the rhythms of its harmonious, natural work. Pictures of this rhythmic work abound, particularly in the last several decades of the nineteenth century. Bernard's superb vision of a buckwheat harvest painted in 1888 shows costumed peasants in simplified gestures, forming the small conical stacks of buckwheat with no visible strain or difficulty. Their work flows easily, as if they are in harmony with nature. Pissarro too was fascinated by the almost easy, natural movement of working peasant figures and his *Peasant Women Setting Props for Peas* of 1890 has all the appearance of a graceful dance in nature. It is interesting, and not irrelevant, to observe that, in spite of the fact that Pissarro believed in a modern agro-industrial

Jacob Becker (1810-1872):
The Storm, 1840.

utopia, his visionary images of work are consistently rural, and he showed no interest in the "artificial" rhythms of urban industrial labour.

Most pictures of the natural rhythms of peasant work concern the planting cycles of agriculture, particularly grain crops, and have deep roots in the European tradition of seasonal landscape painting. Yet, whereas Poussin included a wheat harvest in the background of his summer landscape with Ruth and Boaz in the *Four Seasons* series of 1660–1664, modern painters following Millet were content to show us the harvesters without a difficult biblical reference. Furthermore, it was not only the natural cycles of peasant work that characterized it to the urban mind, but also the collective effort it called for. Nowhere was this

collectivity better represented than in scenes of grain harvests and gleaning. From Millet and Breton in the 1850s, through Lhermitte, Pissarro, and many others in the last decade of the century, the grain harvest was the moment of the year at which natural bounty and collective work came together to express the totality of peasant society. Even the scenes of natural disasters which abound in romantic peasant paintings of the 1840s and 1850s come most often during or just after the bountiful harvest which crowns the agricultural year. In nearly all these pictures of harvesting, the ages and sexes are all present, with women working next to men, and children beside their mothers. In this way, agricultural work is not merely a harmonious integration of man and nature, but also of man with man and

Jules Breton (1827-1906):
Haystack on Fire, 1856.

man with woman. When viewed from the sexually stratified vantage-point of the urban bourgeoisie, for whom these paintings were made, this integration of the sexes in the process of work was remarkable. Travel writers in France, from Arthur Young in the 1780s to Philip Hamerton who came nearly a century later, were fascinated by the sight of women and men working together in the fields. Hamerton, with a painter's eye, described "the labourers... of both sexes, men with bronze arms and breasts and broad straw hats, and women, the rich glow of whose sunburnt faces tells even at a distance, when they rise occasionally out of the green sea of vine leaves wherein they stoop and are hidden." Similar scenes were also recorded by visitors to Spain, Portugal, and Italy.

Julien Dupré (1851-1910):
Haying Scene, 1884.

Jules Bastien-Lepage (1848-1884):
Haymaking, 1878.

82

Léon Lhermitte (1844-1925):
The Noonday Rest, 1905.

Within these almost symphonic images of collective work, there exists another kind of harvest image which dwells on the difficult heroism of peasant labour rather more than it celebrates its joys. Julien Dupré's *Haying Scene* of 1884, one of many such pictures, focuses on a single female worker, separated from the total context of the grain harvest and placed under a troubled sky to work against time. There is an anxious immediacy to the image and a directness which makes it difficult to sympathize with the woman who is utterly oblivious to the viewer and absorbed in her work. To the nineteenth-century bourgeois viewer, she was a woman doing the physical work of a man, and her closest counterparts in nineteenth-century painting are the exhausted laundresses of Degas. This image can be considered in conjunction with the increasingly frequent representations of the exhausted peasant after concentrated bouts of labour. Jules Bastien-Lepage chose to portray an exhausted couple resting in his *Haymaking* of 1878, and Lhermitte painted or drew "noonday rests" on several occasions. Each of these pictures stresses the sheer physicality of labour and makes clear to

the viewer its debilitating effect on the peasant worker; and each of them solved, at least in part, the problem of the careful representation of figures in motion. It is the critic Paul Mantz, in his long descriptive analysis of Bastien-Lepage's picture, who best helps us to understand the complexity of contemporary reactions to these images of rest after work.

"This peasant woman is a monument of sincerity, a type figure one will remember forever. She is deeply browned by the sun, she is ugly; her head is square and rough-hewn; this is the inexorably faithful rendering of a young country woman who has never looked at herself in the mirror of the ideal... But in this ugliness there is a soul. This haymaker so true in her attitude... her eyes fixed on a mysterious horizon, is engrossed in dim thought, in an instinctive reverie whose intensity is deepened by the intoxication induced by the smell of the newly cut grass. The sound of a bell, the call of the foreman, will soon pull her out of her silent contemplation. She will resume her hard labour, she will re-enter the fateful round of real life. But during this strenuous day her spirit will have had its interlude... Of all the pictures in the Salon,

Vincent Van Gogh (1853-1890):
The Reaper (after Millet), 1889.

Mihaly von Munkácsy (1844-1900):
Woman Carrying Faggots, 1873.

including the religious pictures, this composition by Bastien-Lepage is the one most packed with thought."

All these late century pictures of resting peasants have been chosen in preference to better known paintings by Millet to show the extent to which this other attitude to peasant work was as common or typical as the optimistic or progressive view already discussed. The fact that certain artists produced both kinds of paintings testifies to their desire to consider the image of the peasant-as-worker in a complex manner, free from simple ideological constraints. For Millet, Dupré, Lhermitte, and Bastien-Lepage, the very fact that work was hard made its gains so much the sweeter. For them, images of peasant exhaustion were not necessarily negative. Rather, they celebrated the rigours of honest work within the larger sphere of peasant life. Breton catalogued his peasant pictures under the following headings:

(1) work, (2) rest, (3) rural festivals, (4) religious festivals; and this classification indicates that, for him, work was at the root of peasant life and that, in whatever form, peasant labour had to be considered along with both rest and celebration. Millet likewise included rest, prayer, and peasant meals as counterbalancing the cycle of toil; and Bastien-Lepage preferred to represent "the end of work" to "work" itself.

The remainder of the pictures chosen to illustrate peasant labour represent single figures, or two at most, involved in a single task. In this way, they stem from the first and greatest image of peasant labour, Millet's *The Sower*, a painting which Breton called "une sorte d'allégorie du travail de la terre." Because of this isolation of the worker, these pictures possess an emblematic quality and, in considering them, the viewer must confront the working peasant directly. Many of them derive from larger "catalogues" of peasant work like those visual encyclopaedias referred to above (page 77). Yet, unlike their sources, they isolate the specific task from its position in a total work-portrait, so that the meaning and character of that action exists in and of itself. Most of these pictures fall into two broad categories, work with plants and work with animals, and each stresses the intimate bond which exists between the peasant and nature.

The Hungarian artist Munkácsy painted hundreds of peasant genre pictures in the realist tradition and chose, in his *Woman Carrying Faggots*, to raise questions about the relationship between peasants and forests. By 1873, when Munkácsy's picture was made, this subject had been represented already by Millet and numerous other French realists whose work Munkácsy knew, and it would later be taken up by artists as diverse as Pissarro and Segantini. All these pictures place peasants in a corner of

nature which they rarely owned and over which they exercised few rights. They can be compared to contemporary representations of gleaners because each portrays a form of rural charity. In the case of the faggot gatherers, the charity is that of the forester and the wealthy forest owner who, in certain regions, allowed peasants to gather brushwood. In some areas, faggot gathering was prohibited and was therefore only engaged in by those willing to risk punishment (see page 138). Balzac, in his novel *Les Paysans*, described in detail the strained relationship between peasant villagers and the foresters employed by aristocratic landowners, and all this information, literary and historical, lends greater poignancy to Munkácsy's ruggedly painted image of a young female faggot gatherer. We know that she is poor, dependent upon the largesse of unseen individuals, and that she is tired and resting far from home. The

Anton Mauve (1838-1888):
The Kitchen Garden, 1887.

Rosa Bonheur (1822-1899):
Ploughing in the Nivernais: First Dressing, 1849.

intimate accord between peasant and nature so often stressed in the peasant image is eschewed by the artist who chose, by his concentration upon this particular subject, to raise disturbing questions about class distinction and ownership. Indeed, because the painting was intended to be viewed in isolation rather than as part of an encyclopaedia of rural life, it forced the contemporary viewer to confront not only the subject as painted, but also the subject as experienced in life and literature with all its troubling ramifications.

Other painted emblems of rural work with plants are less morally complex than Munkácsy's painting and lend themselves more easily to a Virgilian interpretation. Anton Mauve painted a single female peasant in Holland tending her bean plants with a quiet intensity and self-absorption. She is pretty and gentle, her work at once physically easy and expressive of her complete understanding of the plants she tends. It is, by any standards, appropriate work for a woman and a wonderful subject for an artist interested as much in the rich interplay of greens as in the demands of his subject. The painting

becomes, in a sense, a decoration in which figure and setting are gently interwoven so as to produce an utterly pleasing result.

These pictures of gathering and tending of plants are the tiniest fraction of an immense number of paintings of planters, weeders, harvesters, and gatherers made for sale and exhibition from 1850 until the early twentieth century. They represented the peasant as what Georges Lecomte called "un homme végétal," as a man whose life cycle is analogous to that of the plants he sows, tends, and harvests. Seen in this larger context, Van Gogh's *Reaper* is only one such image, one of a series which is, in itself, part of an endless series devoted to the cyclical work of the agricultural calendar. In many of these pictures, the peasant extends his body by the use of simple tools, and the technics of agriculture, at their most primitive level, fascinated early painters of the peasantry as much as the allegories of work in seasonal time. The sickles, hoes, shovels, and shears were faithfully described by painters of peasant genre, yet among the most powerful tools of the peasant were not metal tools, but animals. The connec-

Rosa Bonheur (1822-1899):
Ploughing Scene, 1854.

tion between human life and animal life is expressed by the relationship between the peasant and his animal: this was a subject addressed over and over by artists who studied the varieties of peasant work.

Perhaps the most common theme depicting this relationship is that of peasants ploughing. There are countless paintings, drawings, and prints which analyse in detail the interworking of man, animal, and tool which is the essence of ploughing. The subject had an even greater significance because it was connected with seasonal agriculture and planting and could therefore serve as an allegory of regeneration through work. It is not by chance that ploughing was the subject of the first important peasant image of post-revolutionary France, Vincent's *Agriculture*, and that it reappeared frequently in the realist tradition, as in Rosa Bonheur's great *Ploughing Scene* of 1854. One of the most famous artists of the mid-nineteenth century inside and outside France, Bonheur specialized not in peasant genre, but in painting of animals, and it was only this aspect of peasant work which fascinated her. Like Loubon in Provence,

she was interested in the motion and muscle strain of animals, precisely the same qualities which had presented such difficulties to painters of peasant workers, and her pictures represent peasants making intelligent use of animals for their brute strength. In them, man, whether peasant or not, triumphs over nature through the use of animals. Yet the emblem of the plougher was too strong to be confined to the realist aesthetic and was used as a symbol of regeneration by Pissarro and many anti-realist painters of peasant life. Segantini approached the subject in a heroic painting, *Ploughing*, of the late 1880s. Picked out in the clear, bright light of an alpine landscape, the plough, guided by one male peasant, is pulled by two horses led by another male peasant facing backwards. This ensemble of men, tool, and animals is placed against a stunning background of snow-covered peaks with a peasant village nestled in the mountainside. The landscape reminds us of the chill of winter and the ruggedness of nature, and the village serves both to localize the painting and to place this emblem of peasant labour in a larger human setting. Hence the

Max Liebermann (1847-1935):
Woman with Goats in the Dunes, 1890.

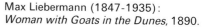

image becomes an epitome of peasant life, at once a celebration of and a submission to the rigours of nature.

Animals were valuable not only for their strength, but also for their coats, their hides, and their meat. They served the peasant as a commodity as well as a tool, and this other aspect of the peasant's relationship to animals in the context of labour is even more common than scenes of ploughing. Pictures of the peasant as a herder or tender of animals abounded largely because of their association with Christian pastoralism, a connection which made them appealing to conservative, "official" society. Millet made perhaps the most important contributions to this subject, often painting young female peasants tending cattle (see page 36), but it was the image of the sheep herder which served an emblematic function more clearly and which was represented many times.

The example illustrated here, Charles Jacque's *Shepherd and Flock*, painted in 1880 and exhibited in the Salon of 1888, represents a

Charles Jacque (1813-1894):
Shepherd and Flock, 1880.

firmly determined shepherd moving through a desolate landscape with his flock. The sheep were carefully painted by an artist whose chief reputation, like Rosa Bonheur's, was as an animal painter. Indeed, the sheep in the foreground possess individual physiological differences and hence different kinds of expression and intelligence which make them almost human. The shepherd is more of a type figure than are his sheep. Yet it is the accord of purpose which unites peasant and animal in Jacque's painting and gives the ensemble a collective meaning.

Peasants were not always so successful with their animals as most pictures of herding and pasturing would have us believe, and there is another sub-genre of peasant paintings in which the peasant and his animals struggle for domination. Such is the subject of Max Liebermann's *Woman with Goats in the Dunes* of 1890. Liebermann represents a sort of tug-of-

war between a peasant woman and a goat which reminds us of the struggle between the peasant girl Françoise and her cow in the opening lines of Zola's novel *La Terre*. One untethered goat trots along amiably, and the other, tied as if in foreknowledge of its disobedience, resists its fate. The peasant woman is not to be outdone, and her determination is expressed by her refusal to turn around to acknowledge the wayward goat. The presence of the broken rope with its bell dangling from the woman's arm makes the meaning of the picture clear. The goats had attempted to stray towards freedom; they failed and are being brought home under the domination of man. In their respective decisions to accept and to rebel against that domination lies the general subject of the painting, and one wonders where Liebermann's sympathies were placed. Or was he raising the more general question of the peasant's domination by or of nature itself?

Family

"Mingling with a rural family, taking their work to heart, sharing their joys and troubles, their hopes and fears, this also means studying a form of human existence to which none of us can be indifferent, so closely does it touch us." Marcel Charlot, who wrote these words at the end of the nineteenth century, believed strongly that peasant life, at its deepest level, was family life, and his book *Paysages et Paysans* not only begins with the above passage but ends with a peasant print by Léon Lhermitte, representing a peasant family of three generations—husband, wife, child, and grandmother—eating their humble meal, and Charlot was moved by it to write: "No more is expected of life than what it can fairly give. Joys and sorrows are shared, and one is proud to see the children grow up, improve in looks, and become a credit to their father and mother."

For Marcel Charlot, as for most Frenchmen of the nineteenth century, family life was the strength of the nation, and respect for parents not only the duty of the child but also a value without which civilization would die. His recommendation that his reader visit a peasant family to experience its joys and sorrows was made at a time when French conservatives were obsessed with declining family values in a rapidly modernizing and urbanizing world, and Charlot, along with many of his contemporaries, looked to the peasant for strong moral direction. The peasant family depicted in his text is typical of many thousands of such families in images, both printed and painted, made to embody the family values so dear to the bourgeoisie. The "eternal" family of the peasant symbolized for them the continuity among generations and the hope for a continued regeneration of enduring values much as images of sowers and reapers symbolized the regeneration of life on the earth. For them, peasant society was a family society, undisturbed by the greed and ambitions which tore at the fabric of bourgeois society.

It goes without saying that real peasant society was not at all like this harmonious familial image, and that the countless paintings of peasants playing with their children, sitting together by the fire, working together in the fields, or preparing their meagre meals were images made in the service of a social ideal; they did not proceed from an analysis of peasant culture itself. Travel writers, novelists, and early critics of peasant culture were almost united in their portrayal of a peasant society directly opposed to this ideal, a diseased society riddled with scheming, squabbling, and treachery, whose only law was individual greed. The peasants of Balzac and Zola thought little of family unity, and a reader of *La Terre* would be hard put to find in that world any of the values extolled by Charlot. While it is probable that these contrary views are unnecessarily bleak, their "anti-idealism" (as Courbet called it) expressed some home truths and served both to undercut the accuracy and show up the symbolism of many pictures of united peasant families.

Once again, the historian confronts what might be called the idealizing condition of the pictorial arts, particularly painting. While in a play, essay or novel it is easy to demonstrate the baseness and greed which motivated peasant family life, these same qualities are difficult to represent in the visual arts without the aid of a text or, at the very least, a narrative sequence of pictures. Peasants, even ugly peasants, were "imaged" so that they could stand as exemplars of some larger truth or moral lesson. Indeed, pictures of familial discord and suspicion are so rare that it is worth including one simply because it is virtually unique. In the mid-1870s Jean-François Raffaëlli painted a large "group portrait" of the generations of the family of Jean-le-Boiteux, Breton peasants from Plougasnou. The brutal realism of his image is extended to the title, and these peasants, far from being an idealized symbolic family, are very real. Although the canvas was cut down on the left, excluding the daughter and part of the father, it retains its brilliantly original composition which tellingly conveys the disunity of the family and the suspicious isolation of the

figures both from each other and from the viewer. This portrait is a kind of peasant version of Degas's *Belleli Family* and, like its source, revels in the psychological discontinuities of modern family life. Its wilful anti-idealism becomes clear when it is compared with other pictures on the same theme.

John Opie's *Peasant Family* is in the tradition of gently pastoral paintings of rural families by English artists of the late eighteenth century like Gainsborough and Morland. Here Opie chose to enlarge and particularize the wife and daughters of an unnamed peasant and to show them at

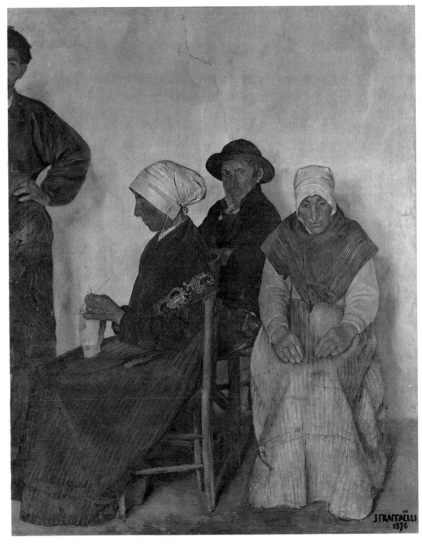

Peter von Hess (1792-1871):
Italian Peasant Family in Tivoli, 1820.

Jean-François Millet (1814-1875):
Man Grafting a Tree, 1855.

Franz von Defregger (1835-1921):
The Visit, 1875.

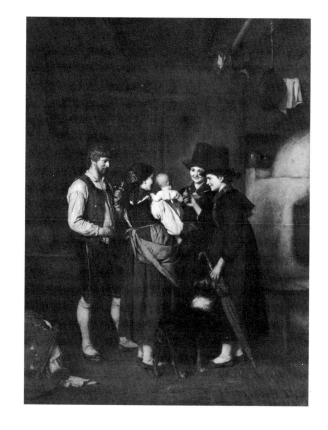

leisure with the family dog. There is no hint of poverty or deprivation, no reference to toil or the physical hardships of rural life. Rather, the bond between mother and child in this barely peasant context is made analogous to the bond between peasant and nature. Peter von Hess was equally idealizing in his *Italian Peasant Family in Tivoli*, painted in 1820. Such scenes of a peasant leaving or returning to his adoring wife and child were to become common later in the nineteenth century. The presence of the donkey, and the Raphaelesque infant, suggest a reference to the flight into Egypt, and the picturesque, decayed peasant dwelling in which this family lives seems to be no more or less squalid than the manger in which Christ was born.

Later pictures of northern peasants are equally laden with symbols. Millet's *Man Grafting a Tree* of 1855 is an extended allegory of continuity and renewal. A young male peasant patiently grafts a live twig from a good apple tree onto the limbs of his old one. His wife and infant child look on with an almost hypnotically rapt

attention. Behind this young couple is an obviously prosperous farmhouse with espalier trees and beehives, all of which complete the various allusions to regeneration through the work of the family. Although Millet makes no overt reference to Christian themes, the painting is no less emblematic, no less profound than that of Peter von Hess. Millet painted many peasant family groups during his career, and all of them stress not so much the continuity between the past and the present, but rather that between the present and the future. The peasants in his family scenes are never old, and there are rarely grandparents or other elders, cousins, aunts, half brothers, or sisters. Indeed, the extended family with numerous children so often associated with real rural culture does not seem to have appealed to nineteenth-century painters of peasant life. Rather, the young, strong couple with one or two infant children was the basic unit in the tradition of paintings representing the peasant family established by Millet and his contemporaries.

The most often-repeated peasant family image of the century, and the one charged with the deepest emblematic significance, is the family meal. The Dutch artist Jozef Israels painted, drew, and etched the subject frequently, and *The Frugal Meal* was among his most famous pictures. The peasant family of father, mother, and three young children eat together with a simple gravity of expression in the darkness of their home. In spite of the presence of a chicken pecking their crumbs, the interior is by no means sordid and the family is arranged in a bilaterally symmetrical composition which lends stability to the group. The family eat without the benefit of silver cutlery, glasses, or China, yet this meal, shared by the mother and father, is the well-earned and satisfying conclusion to their day of work which will become, in time, the work of their children.

Van Gogh, in taking a nearly identical subject, *The Potato Eaters*, imbued it with even greater power and ambiguity. The family chosen by Van Gogh is not the normal unit, but an unusually

Vincent Van Gogh (1853-1890):
The Potato Eaters, 1885.

ambiguous extended family. While it is obvious that there are two couples and a child, it is not clear to whom the child belongs. The hands and faces of the four adult peasants are worn into an almost caricatural image of the hardness of peasant life and they dominate a space which, although accurate in its details, is distorted for expressive purposes. This ordinary peasant meal has been transformed by Van Gogh into a deeply disturbing ritual presided over by a young girl whose face is hidden from us and whose profile is obscured by the steam rising from the potatoes. All is given definition by the light from an old oil lamp hanging directly over the girl's head and there is a sadness and fatalism which permeates the picture. Like so many other peasant pictures, *The Potato Eaters* carries religious meaning as well. An image of the crucifixion appears above the head of the older male peasant on the left, and the entire composition has the air of a biblical supper, with potatoes and a hot grain beverage being the food of the earth and, for Van Gogh, analogous in part to the body and blood of Christ. For all its quirks and spatial distortions, the composition is bilaterally symmetrical and reads clearly from outside to inside, from old age through young adulthood to youth. The young girl, the symbol

Jozef Israels (1824-1911):
The Frugal Meal, exhibited 1876.

Vincent Van Gogh (1853-1890):
Evening (after Millet), 1889.

of the future, has no clear place in Van Gogh's scheme. No one in the painting acknowledges her presence by glance or gesture, and she alone has no chair. Yet, for all her ambiguity, she is the centre of this ritual meal, and her very separation from that milieu raises difficult questions in the viewer's mind about the future of the peasantry and, by extension, about the future of the world.

The layer upon layer of meaning, and the stubbornly difficult quality of Van Gogh's *Potato Eaters*, were countered by the artist in 1889 with a simpler and gentler image of a peasant family called *Evening*. It represents a young peasant couple and their infant seated around the fire after dinner. The interior almost revolves around the source of light, while shadows and inexplicable reflections emanate from it, uniting all the elements, human and otherwise, of this beautiful peasant world. Here Van Gogh expressed the enduring values of family harmony embodied in peasant life and created an image in which light reaches every corner of the room, shedding its blessings and revealing all. The peasant family became for him, as it was for Charlot and so many of their contemporaries, "human existence to which none of us can be indifferent, so closely does it touch us."

Léon Lhermitte (1844-1925):
Christ Visiting the Poor, 1905.

Paul Gauguin (1848-1903):
The Vision After the Sermon: Jacob Wrestling with the Angel, 1888.

Religion

Near the turn of the present century, two artists, a German, Fritz von Uhde, and a Frenchman, Léon Lhermitte, painted nearly identical pictures. In each a peasant family is gathered around a kitchen table for a Sunday meal, and in each there is a visitor from another realm. Christ comes to the peasants not as an apparition, nor as a body surrounded by blinding light, but as a man. If one of the peasants reached out, he could touch Christ, and in each version there is a place for him to sit at the table. Both paintings seem more than faintly ridiculous to us today, and although each was popular during the period of its making they have both passed into obscurity. Yet, in spite of what seems to be their failure as paintings, they serve to remind us of an idea ever present in the nineteenth century: that the peasant was naturally religious. For both Uhde and Lhermitte, Christ was more real to a peasant family than to any other kind of family, and it would be difficult for us to imagine a similar scene in a bourgeois or an aristocratic home. Christ would never have appeared in Paris, and when he does make an urban appearance in the paintings of Ensor, he is the apocalyptic Christ of the Second Coming, not a casual Sunday visitor to a peasant home.

The concreteness of peasant religious experience which Uhde and Lhermitte expressed and the very realism of their treatment can be found in other nineteenth-century paintings as well. Gauguin's *Jacob Wrestling with the Angel* includes the vision of Jacob in the same pictorial realm as the priest and his female peasant parishioners, and Jules Bastien-Lepage gave very real bodies to the celestial voices calling to his famous *Joan of Arc* of 1879. For all these artists, and for many nineteenth-century writers as well, religion was so essential a part of peasant life, utterly immediate and accessible, that there was no division between secular and sacred worlds for the peasant. Indeed, religion, like work and family life, is the third of the four great virtues of peasant culture as defined by the

Ferdinand Waldmüller (1793-1865):
The Harvest, 1846.

Jules Bastien-Lepage (1848-1884):
Joan of Arc, 1879.

peasant image and, like the two already discussed, its expression preoccupied painters from various countries and of various religious affiliations. All three of these virtues are embodied in a highly symbolic early peasant painting by Waldmüller, *The Harvest*, of 1846. Three generations of an Austrian peasant family harvest their wheat beneath their rural shrine with its tiny garlanded crucifixion. We know that their industriousness, their unity, and above all their Catholic piety will protect them from the storm which is brewing in the mountains in the background, and that their harvest will not be spoiled by rain.

Adolph Tidemand (1814-1876):
The Haugian Sect, 1852.

Gustave Courbet (1819-1877):
A Funeral at Ornans, 1850.

clerical Courbet chose to submit a picture of a rural burial in his native town, *A Funeral at Ornans*, to the famous "peasant" Salon of 1850. As with all other rural figure paintings by Courbet, his *Funeral* includes many figures who cannot be classified as peasants, and it addresses itself to rural class stratification as do all the Ornans series. In spite of its blunt realism and frank portrayal of the indifference, even boredom, of many of the figures, it moved many viewers sympathetic to realism and was read by them as an absolutely honest expression of rural piety. That this view is not in line with the artist's intentions is not the point. Rather, the tendency to consider religious experience, even that associated with death, as central to peasant life triumphed in several positive readings of the painting by viewers as diverse as Castagnary and Jules Breton. Indeed, what we have already called the idealizing tendency of painting affected the viewers' reactions to the most realist of rural religious images.

Nineteenth-century pictures of rural piety and religion can be divided into two groups. The first derives from Schnetz and Robert and investigates the nature of religious ritual in peasant society. We are shown peasant processions or church services, and either the "official" or the ethnographic nature of peasant devotion is stressed. These pictures are countered by a second kind of religious image in which peasant prayer and piety have no need of liturgy, vestments, or any of the other trappings of ecclesiastical life, but rather are seen as emerging from the life of the fields. The first kind persists throughout the century, but its greatest works are earlier, stemming directly from the grand history paintings of the classical painters of peasant life. These enormous, multifigural canvases are gradually replaced by smaller, more intimate ones in which individual and family piety is truly the subject. The last painting of the earlier tradition to dominate the imagination of Europe was Jules Breton's *Benediction of the Wheat in Artois*, exhibited at the Salon of 1857. It was perhaps Breton's intention to challenge Robert and Courbet, and to combine the

Adolph Tidemand brought out another side of peasant piety in his rural history painting *The Haugian Sect* of 1852. It represents a group of peasant disciples of Hans Nielson Hauge, a Norwegian lay preacher who was born of a peasant family in the eighteenth century and died in 1824 after a period of imprisonment for ecclesiastical dissent. Hauge was an anti-rationalist theologian known for his attachment to the peasantry whose lives he sought to better not only through religion, but also through improvements in agriculture and peasant industry. The pietist followers of Hauge, as represented by Tidemand, are shown as intensely devoted peasants whose religion had none of the emphasis on celebration seen in pictures of Italian rural Catholicism, but which was equally central to their lives. If Tidemand was considered the northern Léopold Robert, *The Haugian Sect* can be viewed as his *Madonna dell'Arco*, and the stylistic differences between the two paintings lie less in their expression of peasant faith than in the nature of the two painters' religions.

If these two pictures represent the depth of peasant faith in the nineteenth century, they also hint at its range. It is fair to say that there is no great painter of the peasantry, with the exception of the agnostic Pissarro, who did not paint at least one picture devoted to rural religious experience. Even the atheist and fiercely anti-

former's idealized religiousness with the latter's realism of costume, pose, and setting.

Always ready with words, Breton himself described the painting with his customary elegance: "Modern civilization has not had time to disfigure the simple silhouette of a village clustered about its quiet bell-tower, amid a sea of wheatfields... Here they are, the peasants who smiled at me in my childhood. They go their way, walking with a stoop, with shambling steps, murmuring psalms... on they go quietly, in their Sunday best, along this road which has drunk up their sweat and which, in this holiday sunshine, seems also to change with its thousands of blossoming flowers... on they go, craving for their home no more than unruffled happiness, than daily bread earned by labour, than health and honour. On they go, thanking Providence whose image they piously follow, in this monstrance which shines in the sunlight."

Jules Breton (1827-1906):
Benediction of the Wheat in Artois, 1857.

Wilhelm Leibl (1844-1900):
Three Women in Church, 1878-1882.

In Breton's rosy memories there is no hint of discord among the peasants, of the squabbling about payment for the priest which often accompanied such rituals. Nor does he enlighten us about the ecclesiastical nature of the procession, though it seems to represent a rural religious custom which has no relation to the official liturgy of the Catholic Church. What is important, however, is that Breton chose his subject precisely because of its attachment to the work of the fields which was, for him, the focus of rural life. Priests and villagers are united in the procession just as God and agriculture go hand in hand. It is no accident that Breton does not name the divinity in his text, but talks instead of Providence as if to underscore the very pantheism of peasant religious experience.

The tendency to emphasize personal rather than institutional piety in peasant pictures characterized the second half of the nineteenth

Jean-François Millet (1814-1875):
The Angelus, 1857-1859.

century, but did not hold for the many paintings of religious festivals, particularly the pardons of Brittany which fill the 1880s and 1890s and which form part of the ethnographic aspect of the peasant image discussed earlier. These pardons were painted not so much to exemplify rural piety as to document regional customs, and the close attention paid in them, by artists from Boudin to Dagnan-Bouveret, to the niceties of costume and pose indicates clearly that the depiction of rural religious fervour was not their primary aim. If one looks through the annals of late nineteenth-century painting of peasant religious experience in the context of institutional religion, it is Wilhelm Leibl's *Three Women in Church*, painted around 1880, which best serves as an example of the new image of personal piety. Where Schnetz, Robert, Courbet, and Breton show us dozens of figures and paint a complete documentation of a ritual event, Leibl, like Laboulaye in his *At the Sermon* and Dagnan-Bouveret in *The Consecrated Bread*,

100

Jozef Israels (1824-1911):
Their Daily Bread
(The Shepherd's Prayer), 1864.

omitted from his limited visual field all but the worshippers themselves. There is no priest, no altar, no religious image, no incense. By focusing his attention on three female worshippers, Leibl is able to examine almost clinically what might be called the progressive stages of religious experience in the nineteenth century. The peasant woman on the far left gazes with rapt attention at the unseen priest or religious image. Her hands are folded in prayer, and it is clear from the juxtaposition to her companions that she is unable to read. The next worshipper clutches an old Bible or service book and she bends her head away from the unseen image in her attempt to decode the text. The third figure, younger than her companions and dressed in a splendidly embroidered costume and a jaunty spring hat, looks at her prayer book, which is at once smaller and newer than that of the reading worshipper sitting next to her. Her fingers seem to mark several places in the text at once and she is about to turn the page. By his focus on these three worshippers, all unaware of the viewer's presence, Leibl raised questions about the education and aspirations of peasants and, by his exclusion of male figures or children, about the breadth of peasant religion.

The most moving and most frequent image of peasant piety during the second half of the century consists of worship in connection with labour in the fields. The quiet prayers of peasants out of doors in the midst of an almost holy nature were represented by artists from Breton and Millet to Israels and Lhermitte. In describing the observation which prompted his painting *Women Weeding the Fields,* Breton makes clear that it was their work which connected them with God, not the Church. "In the self-communion of the silent hour, the unutterable goodness of things aroused a thrill of religious awe... It was like a natural transfiguration of the humblest of labours. Nowhere have I felt closer to God, nowhere have I better understood that work is a prayer."

This passage applies equally well to many other pictures, from Millet's emblematic representation of peasant piety in *The Angelus* to Jozef Israels' *Their Daily Bread.* In each a man and his wife are represented in an act of devotion, not in church, but in the fields. For Millet, they are bent together in silent prayer at the end of the day; for Israels, the young shepherd gives thanks to God for his daily bread as his wife prepares his mid-day meal. These pictures, as well as their numerous reproductions and versions, embody an idea of religion as an integral part of work and life rather than something founded on liturgy or doctrine. Collectively, they tell us that peasant man, the most basic of men, lives his life in the service of God.

Patriotism

In 1865 the greatest living Czech painter, Josef Mánes, began work on his masterpiece, the painted decorations for the clock on the exterior of the old town hall in Prague. Built in the fifteenth century, this clock was among the principal symbolic monuments of the old city, and its decoration became an event of political as well as aesthetic significance both for Mánes and the Czech people. Choosing to ignore the classical allegories invented by the previous decorator of the clock-face in the eighteenth century, he created a new symbolic system based on the cycle of the months as embodied in Czech peasant agriculture. For him, the modern viewer in Prague would experience, in the condensed urban time of a half day, the entire year of peasant time, and would hence be reminded, every time he looked at the clock, of the unending labour of the fields. Mánes' intention was to provide in his pictures a new link between the capital city of Prague and its natural territory, Czechoslovakia, rejecting outright the political allegiance to the Austro-Hungarian Empire which had ruled Czechoslovakia from a distance for more than a century. He realized that the most powerful of national symbols for a nation dispossessed of itself was its peasantry.

Although trained in Munich, Josef Mánes instinctively rejected German culture and was appalled to realize as a student that his country, with its own territory and native tongue, was held in bondage by the Habsburgs and that the Czech nobility, upper middle-class, and clergy had allowed themselves to be germanized. Indeed, Mánes became a national hero as the leader of an association of Czech artists and intellectuals who attempted to compel the Emperor Franz Josef to grant the nation its own constitution. After participating in the Czech revolution of 1848, Mánes began to understand that only peasants could keep patriotism alive, and in that conviction he made the first of his trips through Moravia and Slovakia to study and depict the peasant life of his country. He enriched his knowledge of the peasantry not only by visual study, but also by collecting folklore, dances, and songs. His peasant pictures must be read as the principal symbols for a great nationalist movement in all the arts and crafts. He illustrated nationalist songs and painted regional costume studies. More than any other artist of the nineteenth century, he placed the rural image in the service of an explicit political ideology. The peasants on the great clock at Prague united for him reality, poetry, and myth in a synthetic experience of national pride.

Mánes was not alone in this endeavour, for not only was he surrounded by a group of like-minded artists, writers, and composers in Czechoslovakia, but similar groups of intellectuals banded together in other parts of Europe which were ruled from afar. It was natural for painters in Czechoslovakia, Poland, and parts of Russia to conceive of landed peasants as symbols for their nationalist struggles, and most eastern European peasant paintings must be read as part of the nationalist movements in those countries. It is perhaps more difficult for us today to understand the patriotic meanings of many rural images in countries like France, Germany, and Austria, and yet this aspect of the cultural meaning of the peasant image was equally strong in those nations.

Curiously, the peasant image served two patriotic functions in these older, self-ruled nations. First, the peasant as a kind of Everyman was considered, especially in France and Germany, to be the root or base of the nation because he was born there and worked the land with his hands and body. Textual evidence for this view can be found in French Romantic intellectuals like Michelet and George Sand, and in much of the propaganda of the Second Empire. It was a well-known and often repeated fact to a Frenchman that France, much more than Germany or England, was a rural nation and that two-thirds of its population could be classified as peasants. This fact became the basis of the peasant image in a highly popular

Josef Mánes (1820-1871):
Painted Face of the Great Clock, Old Town Hall, Prague, begun 1865.

Second Empire novel by Erckmann-Chatrian called *Histoire d'un Paysan*, a fictional portrayal of the rise of a peasant family from obscurity to a point at which one of its members becomes the president of France. Even Marcel Charlot reminded his readers, as late as 1898, that all Frenchmen, no matter what their present stature, had peasant blood in their veins. Although perhaps connected more closely with Republican nationalism after the French Revolution, these same ideas were expressed by several generations of Romantic nationalists in Germany as well, and formed a large part of the conceptual framework for the pictures of Austrian artists like Reinhold and Waldmüller, each of whom was perceived as a patriotic depicter of his national *Volksleben*. It is fair to say, however, that no French, German, or Austrian artist painted an overtly nationalist image with the conceptual strength of Mánes' great clock in Prague. Indeed, both France and Germany continued to be symbolized by classically dressed, ideal female figures throughout the nineteenth century. Rather, the general idea of a symbolic nationalism rooted in peasant life forms a deep layer of meaning in many peasant paintings. By an early date, peasant images were easily accepted by government-sponsored exhibitions in spite of their realism, precisely because there was such a strong undercurrent of national patriotism in their meaning.

The most problematic and profound aspect of patriotism in the western European peasant image has more to do with the growing regionalist movements in Germany and France than with nationalism. This is particularly true in France, whose national unity has never been as strong as foreigners assume it to be. The political system which is today called regionalism, and which became a powerfully articulate, nationally organized force only at the end of the nineteenth century, was based on nineteenth-century neo-regionalist movements, particularly those in Brittany and Provence. The word regionalism itself was coined in 1874 by a Provençal poet and disciple of Mistral, Berluc-Perussis, as the direct result of a strong regeneration in artistic and literary circles of Provençal as opposed to French culture. Artists contributed widely to this movement, with the result that many of their greatest paintings remain little known today because they are not in Paris and were not sold on the international art market. Indeed, the gradual strengthening of regional art education throughout Europe in the nineteenth century has not been given serious enough treatment by art historians for us to understand fully the role of the peasant image in their regional centres. Paintings like Auguste Herlin's *Threshing Colza on the Lille Plain* of the early 1860s is so rigorously exact in its regional title that the image functions, at least in part, as a documentation of regional rather than national peasant culture. This regional specificity can be found in many other peasant pictures in which the titles give us the exact location of the scenes, and these titles seem to link the peasant figures more to their particular landscape than to the earth itself. Thus they become not so much "everyman" as "regional man." Another famous picture of regional culture which projects its patriotic values is Gustave Brion's *Vosges Peasants Fleeing before an Invasion* of 1867. These

Gustave Brion (1824-1877):
Vosges Peasants Fleeing before an Invasion, 1867.

Alsatian peasants prefer to abandon their village rather than be dominated by a foreign power, in this case Prussia. For Brion, regional culture is subjected to national pressures and, as part of a national propaganda campaign launched by Napoleon III just before the Prussians gathered power for their retaking of Alsace in 1870, he forthrightly depicts Alsace as a French province.

These two French peasant paintings with regional subjects are enough to show that the regional movements which they served were not united in their aims. Some regionalists preferred "region" to "nation," and many people in Provence or Brittany smarted as much under French rule as Mánes in Czechoslovakia did under Austrian rule. Although there are peasant pictures which served this extremist cause, most seem to have been more moderate in their aims, preferring to glorify "region" as part of "nation" and conceiving of regional identity within the general frame of national life. The regionalist movement which developed in the twentieth century reversed the traditional nationalist order of individual allegiance first to God, then to nation, and developed a hierarchy with the individual at the top followed by the community,

the region, and lastly the nation. In many ways the peasant image, with its emphasis on family and community life, served to reinforce in advance these early twentieth-century systems of allegiance, and the staggering number of peasant pictures whose titles reveal regionalist sympathies suggests that many of them, too, were part of the wave of local studies produced by the regionalist movement in the last years of the nineteenth century.

Again, the peasant image has served to fortify a system of values whose origins lay outside peasant culture itself. The regionalist movement can be seen, at least in part, as a reaction against the industrial capitalism which, by the end of the nineteenth century, had swept through northern Europe, disrupting the delicate framework of interwoven regional economic systems. For those whose lives and fortunes were caught up in this economic revolution, the image of the peasant was not simply a symbol of the enduring values of work, family, and religion, but also a reminder of the bond between man and his own *coin de terre* or *pays natal*, a bond which had, for a good percentage of the European population, been broken.

EROTICISM AND INNOCENCE:
Sex and Love in the Peasant Image

Painters have been fascinated by peasant sexuality at least since the seventeenth century. From the rowdy love-making in Rubens' *Kermesse* and the alluring or lascivious figures in Dutch seventeenth-century rural genre paintings, to the innocent erotic scenes in the barnyards and gardens of Boucher and Fragonard, peasants have been pictured as frank indulgers in what we now call free love, and the quick toss in the hay with a peasant girl was seen as part of the erotic education of any young gentleman of the period. This idea of the peasant as instinctively bawdy was given currency in the eighteenth century by a series of sexually charged "rural" novels, culminating in the pseudo-autobiographical novels of Restif de La Bretonne who, as a peasant youth, seemed to have engaged in or thought about little else than sex and whose exploits by the age of ten would have elicited admiration even from Casanova. Nineteenth-century writers were more inhibited in their treatment of such matters. The frank sexuality of the peasant was underplayed by Romantic novelists like George Sand and Erckmann-Chatrian, and returned in full force only with the publication in 1887 of Zola's *La Terre*, a book filled with an almost animal sexuality. By and large, the nineteenth century, whether in Victorian England, post-revolutionary France, or Germany and Austria, treated sexuality with a good deal less frankness than in the past, and perhaps only in peasant genre painting could actual human sexuality be

Wilhelm Rieder (1796-1880):
Girl Selling Pears, 1845.

William Bouguereau (1825-1905):
The Broken Pitcher, 1891.

examined without serious breaches of aesthetic decorum. The depiction of peasant love and sexuality took essentially two forms in nineteenth-century painting: the first, an almost voyeuristic portrayal of the vulnerability and seductiveness of the peasant girl, young and as yet unspoiled by the ravages of rural labour; the second, a more moralistic treatment of rural courtship.

There was a virtual obsession with young and pretty peasant women in the pictorial arts throughout the nineteenth century. The vast majority of figures in peasant painting of that century are women, and of these the majority are unattached, at least in the picture, to a male. It is often the most beautiful of the peasants in a group who engages the viewer's eye, and when peasants are portrayed singly they are, more often than not, pretty young women. This pictorial devotion to the fairer sex has its parallels in travel literature in which illustrations and descriptive passages devoted to rural life treat the peasantry as if more than three-quarters of its population were young and female. One particularly eloquent traveller, H. T. Tuckerman, writing about Italy in the 1840s, considered "female beauty and fine weather" to be the goals of every traveller. The conjunction of these two attractions, he went on to say, "imparts a charmed life to the traveller's experience," and reading further in his text one finds that the most "accessible" of beautiful females were peasants. "Two peasant girls were gaily arrayed and decked with flowers. I have seldom seen more perfect specimens of rural beauty." Specimens they were, in hundreds of travel accounts and innumerable pictures. Peasant men seldom wore the costumes pictured again and again in nineteenth-century illustrated books, and, if nineteenth-century painters refrained from the more explicit sexuality of Rubens or Boucher, their very adoration of the female peasant has a strong element of sexuality as the viewer is asked to gaze longingly at these ever-recurring specimens of rural beauty.

Loving representations of superbly costumed rural "beauties" form a major corpus of peasant pictures from the 1820s, when Schnetz, Robert, and Vernet began the tradition of the idealized peasant portrait, to the end of the nineteenth century. Although we know of no study of the early sale of these pictures, the nineteenth-century literature devoted to Robert and Schnetz hints strongly that they were produced for ready sale and were considered by their makers to be secondary in importance to the multifigural Salon paintings on moral themes. If this supposition is true, and there are many reasons to suspect that it is, the tradition of the "specimen" portrait of the female peasant lasted throughout the century because of its marketability to male purchasers, and perhaps only Millet, of the great painters of the peasantry, failed to cater for this market. Examples of this safely erotic kind of painting are so numerous that full analysis is impossible, and we will illustrate only a few as evidence both of the range and, in certain hands, of the ambiguity of what were specimens of rural beauty. Most often, they represent an isolated female figure, and she generally looks, often piteously, straight into the viewer's eyes. In some cases, she is placed in an awkward or dangerous situation and seems to implore the viewer to save her from her plight. In an alarming number of cases, she is barely an adolescent, and the fact that these nubile peasant girls were painted by artists throughout Europe suggests that the exploiting of sexual innuendoes was more than a Victorian phenomenon.

In 1845 Wilhelm Rieder devoted his considerable talents as a painter to a *Girl Selling Pears* which represents an extremely alluring peasant girl, her head tilted provocatively to one side, her shawl discarded, and her dress pulled down to reveal her shoulders. Like many young girls painted by Rieder and others, she is selling her produce, which is arranged meagrely in the foreground, and she appeals to the viewer to aid her in her poverty. Similar pictures can be found throughout Europe, particularly during the second half of the century, but in France they became the specific province of William Bouguereau. The number of such paintings by Bouguereau is enormous and they range from provocative young girls lying in wheatfields as a storm brews ominously in the background, to pretty girls who have somehow wandered into the thistles and are in need of help. *The Broken Pitcher* of 1891 is at once beautifully constructed and appallingly exploitative of its subject. This peasant girl has gone to the well and broken her vase. The symbolism, if one can use such a grand word in this case, is obvious. What is perhaps most interesting about Bouguereau's erotic peasant girls is the extent to which each painting contains within it a warning of the consequences of free sexuality. There is gener-

Camille Corot (1796-1875):
*Peasant Girl at the Spring
(Girl with the Red Waist)*, 1860-1865.

ally something wrong which either has happened or will happen and the viewer is, in this way, politely reproached for his lascivious intentions. The image allows for both lust and guilt.

The two paintings by Rieder and Bouguereau represent a particularly common type of peasant image in its purest form. There are, however, many others which approach the peasant girl with somewhat more subtle intentions. Corot's late figure paintings are given over fervently to the young female figure in isolation; yet, for Corot, and for his viewer, she is more a muse than a victim of some concocted plight and, if she does have erotic associations, they are less obviously central to the meaning of the picture. His *Peasant Girl at the Spring* makes use of obvious symbolic associations similar to those of Bouguereau. But the jug is not broken; the girl is turned from the viewer, and there is consequently neither engagement nor guilt associated with our admiration of this beautifully costumed peasant girl. This is true as well for the young peasant women, either isolated or in pairs, painted by Pissarro in the early 1880s. These young women are vulnerable to us, the viewer. They are alone. They usually sit or lie on the ground, and we see them from above. Although they never engage our gaze directly, they are clearly present to be admired in their often contorted positions of rest, and there is an unmistakable element of eroticism about them in spite of the fact that they are fully and properly clothed. Pissarro, like his teacher Corot, approached this kind of "saleable" painting with some hesitation. Yet, however chaste, however ambiguous, and however important within the history of modern art these paintings are, they nevertheless fit into a prevailing nineteenth-century type.

It would be wrong to confine this discussion too insistently to France, and for purposes of comparison one should examine two other examples of these rural beauties. For Hugh

Camille Pissarro (1830-1903):
The Rest, Young Peasant Woman Lying on the Grass, 1882.

Cameron, painting in the 1850s, the pretty peasant girls talking together in *Going to the Hay* are not exactly erotic or "available" to the viewer. Yet their very isolation and the fullness of their youth and beauty are remarkable and force us to classify this painting not as a genre description of rural work, but as a celebration of female beauty within the rural world. Segantini, in his beautiful *Girl of the Grisons at the Fountain* of 1887, isolates a costumed young girl against a green field. As in so many of these paintings, she is at "the source" and, this time, drinks from one of the three waterspouts protruding ominously into the pictorial space from the right. The picture is ambivalent again,

Giovanni Segantini (1858-1899):
Girl of the Grisons at the Fountain, 1887.

Hugh Cameron (1835-1918):
Going to the Hay, 1858-1859.

neither a costume study nor a genre painting, and because the girl is unaware of our presence we are allowed the luxury of long adoration as she drinks the pure water which drips down her hand onto her billowing sleeve.

This series of paintings devoted to the titillation of the male spectator raises many more questions about the nature of bourgeois sexuality in the nineteenth century than it does about the peasantry and, as in almost all the manifestations of the peasant image discussed in this book, the peasant is "erotic" in ways associated

— Comme je les aime!.....

Le Benjamin de la mère Roussel et le petit loup de Mam'zelle Rose.

with the systems of sexual restraint and class hierarchy prevailing in urban Europe. All of these pictures relate, either overtly or subliminally, to their viewers and are therefore not to be read as genre scenes. But there is another class of paintings dealing with the customs and manners of peasant love and courtship which make no such demands upon the presence—implied or otherwise—of a male, bourgeois viewer. These are multifigural genre scenes which purport to describe the love of peasants, pictures which are considerably more chaste than their seventeenth- and eighteenth-century proto-types. In fact, with minor exceptions there are few frank representations of peasant sexuality in the nineteenth century. Rather, painters, par-ticularly in Germany and Austria, investigated what might be called the mechanics of rural courtship in pictures which are filled with moral lessons for their bourgeois viewers. Perhaps only in several popular images like Damourette's *How I love them!* of 1853 are peasants allowed

to be leeringly lascivious. Generally, even in popular images, peasant love is a discreet, offstage affair.

In 1820 Heinrich Dähling painted a small study of rural courtship called *At the Garden Fence*. Placed in a setting filled with moral and actual barriers to the free expression of their physical love, a young peasant couple engage in their discreet dalliance in the presence of the young man's elderly father. One knows that the gate in the fence between them, guarded by the father, will remain closed until the wedding. Yet the watering can in the foreground, and the fact that the father is planting tiny new plants, give us hope that their union will not only occur but bear fruit as well. Remote from those of Rubens or Boucher, Dähling's peasants are rather like proper bourgeois, anxious to behave in such a way as to avoid the moral sanctions of society. The peasant image, in this case, makes use of a courtship image to embody the intertwined virtues of work, religion, and family.

112

LES PAYSANS

10

Attend sa Dulcinée.

Abel Damourette:
The Peasants:
(1) *How I love them!*
(2) *Old Mrs Roussel's youngest boy has taught Miss Rose a thing or two.*
(3) *Waiting for his sweetheart.*
Lithographs, 1853.

Heinrich Dähling (1773-1850):
At the Garden Fence, 1820.

William Holman Hunt (1827-1910):
The Hireling Shepherd, 1851.

Moral instruction was no less a part of the intention of the English painter William Holman Hunt in his masterpiece of 1851, *The Hireling Shepherd*. Although at first glance the painting is a charmingly frank portrayal of the beginnings of what will undoubtedly be physical love, the landscape, with the herd of the inattentive shepherd wandering into the wheatfield, makes it clear that the consequences of their pleasure are considerable and that this rural Adam and Eve are playing with the same fate that was, for Hunt's England, the fate of all human beings. No matter how convincing his conjoining of "female beauty" and "fine weather," the end will not be so pretty.

This moralism is also a crucial component of the most sustained pictorial investigation of rural courtship in the mid-nineteenth century, that of Ferdinand Waldmüller. *The Neighbours*, of 1859, represents a peasant couple almost entwined in a passionate embrace. Yet we know by the presence of the fence which is, in itself, entwined with branches and flowers, that they are not married, that she is at home in the barnyard, that he has come from somewhere else, and that their embraces will be frustrated at this point. Again, as with Dähling and many other nineteenth-century paintings of rural courtship, including Bastien-Lepage's 1883 Salon picture *Village Love*, which almost seems like a remaking of *The Neighbours*, fences and other barriers separate man from woman until marriage breaks them down. Waldmüller's moralism is always present in his rural genre painting. In *The Admonition* of 1846, a mother scolds her blushing daughter who has just come back from the fields while water from the nearby well runs over the top of the pitcher she has been filling. In a later painting, *The Rustic Lovers* of 1863, a mother looks askance as her daughter moves into the arms of a young, virile peasant

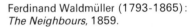

Ferdinand Waldmüller (1793-1865):
The Neighbours, 1859.

Ferdinand Waldmüller (1793-1865):
Waiting For Her (Sunday Morning), 1860.

male. In *Waiting For Her* (or *Sunday Morning*), a young peasant girl clutching her prayer book on her way to church enters a secluded glen where a young man waits for her with flowers. Waldmüller makes her path a rocky and treacherous one, and we know that she may be startled into falling in every sense of the word. Indeed, the paths even of peasant love are filled with gates and barriers, rocky passages and broken bridges, and, what might at first seem to be the innocent joy of rural love-making, has its darker side in nineteenth-century images of rural courtship. We are reminded, in looking at them, of the number of "mistakes" made by young peasant women in eighteenth- and nineteenth-century rural novels. The "paysanne pervertie" of Restif de La Bretonne became an urban prostitute and both Hetty in George Eliot's *Adam Bede* and Thomas Hardy's Tess were themselves portrayed as the unfortunate but guilty parties in intensely dramatic conclusions to novels devoted at first to the joys of rural love. Again, scenes of simple peasant love and courtship without the biblical burdens of guilt and moral sanctions are so rare that we may conclude by illustrating one, Wilhelm Leibl's *In the Country Parlour*, painted about 1890. Leibl shows us a bearded peasant sitting close to a pretty young woman. They chat amiably and look with a frank, earnest simplicity into each other's eyes. There are no hints in the picture of the fall which comes inevitably in love.

Wilhelm Leibl (1844-1900):
In the Country Parlour, c. 1890.

Angelo Morbelli (1853-1919):
For Eighty Centimes, 1895.

THE PAST VERSUS THE PRESENT:
The Peasant in the Modern World

Will progress kill poetry?
Will we have to go into mourning for country life?

Marcel Charlot

For many, indeed for most, painters and writers devoted to the description of country life in the nineteenth century, the peasant inhabited a timeless realm. The rhythms of his life were those of the seasons and the cycle of the agricultural year, and he was unaffected, to a large extent, by the drama of technological change and class conflict which came with the rise of industrial capitalism in Europe. The coincidence between the increased modernization of European life and the rise of the peasant image in the same period has been noted by many writers and has been an undercurrent in all our remarks about the peasant image as the embodiment of enduring moral values at a time of change. Yet it was also recognized very early that peasants too were being forced to alter their rural cultures, that their lives too were subject to the same pressures of change as those of city-dwellers. Some peasants, paid for both their labour and their produce, were petty capitalists, able to work not just on the land but also in the marketplace and, therefore, to make improvements in their clothes and houses. Peasants were conscripted in large numbers into the army and travelled throughout the world in their country's service. The rural world was increasingly affected by tourism and mechanical industrialization as railway and canal networks expanded dramatically throughout Europe. Peasant agriculture was altered not only by small improvements in ploughs and hand tools, but also by the invention of large scale

Léon Lhermitte (1844-1925):
The Harvesters' Wages, 1882.

mechanized harvesting and processing machinery. All these and other elements of the pressures of the present on the timeless world of the peasant can be found in peasant pictures. Although less numerous than those of the eternal peasant cut off from the modern world, these pictures were made throughout the century in practically every European country.

At the Exposition Universelle of 1889 in Paris, Léon Lhermitte exhibited a large painting called *The Harvesters' Wages*. Using the same models he had employed for *The Harvest*, his Salon painting of 1883, he depicted a group of day-labouring peasants, both men and women, in the courtyard of a large and prosperous farm being paid for their work. Their exhaustion and implicit homelessness are made more poignant by the fact that they are juxtaposed against several sheaves of grain which they have harvested, but which they do not own. Indeed, in painting the picture, Lhermitte raised disturbing questions about the relationship between physical labour and private property, questions which had been at the core of a potent political

debate in France since they were raised by Proudhon and Thiers in the 1840s. Yet the real accomplishment of the painting was its frank acceptance of the peasant, or a certain kind of peasant at least, as a member of the working class, as one of a larger society rewarded not in kind, but with cash. The Italian painter Angelo Morbelli raised the same questions a scant six years later in his famous painting *For Eighty Centimes*. Morbelli addressed the issue of money not in the image itself, but in its title, and by juxtaposing in our minds the physical work of a group of anonymous peasant women in the heat of a June day with the fact that they were to be paid so little, he makes the message clear.

Neither of these paintings made at the very end of the century is concerned with the peasant image as a conveyor of "eternal" moral values. Rather, they each present a situation of social ambiguity to an audience unaccustomed to such demands from rural images. In this way, they are realist in a social if not a stylistic sense. Indeed, Morbelli's picture owes a good deal in its strongly modernist geometric structure to the anti-realist aesthetic of post-Impressionism. Nevertheless, it was meant to be taken by the viewer as real, as presenting an actual scene with as much aesthetic force as possible. Such was not always the case with nineteenth-century pictures of the interaction of the "eternal" peasant world with the urban world beyond its limited realm, and this final chapter will explore some of the ways in which the peasant image made peace with modernization. Most works illustrated in this chapter, whether they represent the peasant and war, the interaction between bourgeois and peasant, or the peasant at the marketplace, make every attempt to establish a social as well as a pictorial harmony of these complex subjects and many of them seem to suggest that, because peasants are good, they ought to remain as it was thought they always were, untouched by the modern world, but always working, always patriotic, and always religious.

War and Conscription

It has long been known that European armies were commanded by the upper classes and manned by the lower classes, and that the peasantry largely accounted for the military strength of a nation. The peasant image during the nineteenth century paid its tribute to this fact. The Salons of the 1820s contained no inconsiderable number of pictures representing what Thiers, in his *Salon de 1822*, and others as well, called "soldats-laboureurs." Indeed, Vigneron, in that Salon, submitted a painting made in 1818 of a peasant who, when ploughing his field, turned up skulls with the soil, and the painter-lithographer Charlet repeatedly treated the theme of the return of the peasant-soldier to his village, often to find his farm taken away or his sweetheart married to another. Likewise, there are other genre paintings of the 1820s

Nicolas-Toussaint Charlet (1792-1845):
The Soldier's Burden, 1820.

The Departure and Return of the Conscript.
French popular print (Image d'Epinal), 1875.

Ferdinand Waldmüller (1793-1865):
Leave-Taking of a Conscript, 1858.

which represent peasant families moving into the city, and Charlet's *Soldier's Burden* relates closely to a similar Vernet; both make clear by costume that the depopulation of the countryside which they represent is a depopulation of former soldiers. Many of these pictures force us to read them as indictments of war as we recognize its disastrous effects on humble citizens. Yet their gentle negativism is countered by a larger number of paintings and popular prints in which the conscription and subsequent return of peasants from war is a happy, idealized affair.

In 1820 Peter Krafft made a pair of paintings representing the departure and return of a militiaman from military service. The departure

Peter Krafft (1780-1856):
The Return of the Militiaman, 1820.

relates strongly to prototypes by Greuze; and the return, set in the barnyard, shows a young peasant father reunited with his family, the children grown and healthy, the loving wife still there, and his elderly father alive to share stories of his son's adventures. The style is neo-classical and, like many paintings in that style, it attempts to describe a noble virtue. Indeed, there was a considerable literature in German devoted to the fact that peasants made excellent soldiers because of their manliness, strength, industry, and diligence, values which were thought to be the opposite of the laziness of their urban counterparts. Peasants were seen as the defenders of the fatherland in many books and articles published in Germany in the last decade of the eighteenth century and the first part of the nineteenth, and this image of the peasant-soldier was a strong one in German culture throughout the century. Waldmüller's *Leave-Taking of a Conscript* of 1858 represents a strong, handsome young peasant bidding farewell to a loving family as his girlfriend listens at the side of the picture. Although the sequel of the picture is not made clear, it must be read as one of many such farewells which were balanced by analogous returns, usually with happy results: the peasant saw the world, defended his country, and returned to his rural home to serve it again through labour in the fields. In France the *images d'Epinal* of the mid-nineteenth century repeatedly represent "La Vie du Conscrit," illustrating the cycle of departure, loyal service, wounding, recovery, return, marriage, and fathering a family, a cycle not so very dissimilar from that of a season or a year. Indeed, in contrast to many of the anti-war images produced by the French after the Napoleonic wars, those of the Germans and the later French images tend to stress the natural rhythms of conscription and to act, again, as embodiments of the virtue of patriotism.

Sir David Wilkie (1785-1841):
*Sir Walter Scott
(The Abbotsford Family)*, 1817.

The Peasant and his "Betters": Images of Class Interaction

In October 1817, after a period of study in Paris, the Scottish artist David Wilkie painted what his friend Sir Walter Scott called "a group of south country peasants supposed to be concocting a merry-making." Actually with one exception, these were not peasants at all, but Sir Walter Scott himself with his family. A description of the painting by an early student of Wilkie's will serve to decode the complex image. "The sitting figure, in the dress of a miller, represents Sir Walter Scott, author of a few score of volumes and proprietor of Abbotsford in the county of Roxburgh. In the front, and representing a country wag somewhat addicted to preaching, stands Sir Adam Ferguson, knight-keeper of the regalia of Scotland. In the background is a very handsome old man upwards of eighty-four years old at the time, painted in his own character as a shepherd. He also belongs to the numerous clan of Scott. Of the three female figures, the eldest is the late regretted mother of the family represented. The young person most forward in the group is Miss Sophia Charlotte Scott, now Mrs. John Gibson Lockhart; and the other is her sister Miss Anne Scott. Both are represented as ewe milkers with their milk pails. On the left hand of the shepherd, the young man holding the fowling piece is the eldest son of Sir Walter, now captain in the King's Hussars. The boy is the youngest of the family, Charles Scott, now of Brasenose College, Oxford."

Although there are many eighteenth-century portraits of Englishmen in the country, some shown against agricultural scenes, there is no major precedent for this picture in which a famous and wealthy intellectual chooses to have himself, his family, and friends painted *as peasants*. The Scottish nationalism of Scott can stand as a partial explanation of the portrait, but it is easier to read it as a complex, unsettling, and aesthetically unresolved investigation of the

Wilhelm von Kobell (1766-1853):
Horseman and Two Peasant Girls, 1829.

growing rapprochement between the upper classes, however defined, and the peasantry. As the nineteenth century continued and the peasant image in art and literature flourished, peasants were imbued increasingly with positive values and confronted with greater social familiarity by members of the upper classes. Sir Walter Scott here becomes a peasant storyteller, giving himself the attributes of directness and honesty of these "natural" raconteurs. Yet there is a kind of double "merry-making" in the picture, whose very artificiality casts some doubt on its sincerity, and it is to another small group of pictures representing the frank interaction of bourgeois and peasant that we must turn for clarification of nineteenth-century notions of class interaction.

It must first be said that the great majority of nineteenth-century peasants in image and word exist quite apart from their larger society. There are *no* bourgeois or aristocratic figures in the rural genre paintings of Waldmüller, Liebermann, Millet, or Lhermitte; and even artists like Pissarro or Bastien-Lepage, who painted both urban and rural environments, kept them, for the most part, rigorously separate. Only in the rural novels of Balzac, George Eliot, Flaubert, and others is there any literary investigation of the peasant in the context of a larger society, and with the exception of George Eliot's or Thomas Hardy's novels, there is not much real interaction in rural fiction except between servants and masters. The conversations between peasant and property-owner in Balzac's *Les Paysans* are stilted and unconvincing; when one finishes the novel, one is inclined to think that peasants should remain in their place and be viewed from a distance. Such is also the general message of the paintings and prints which represent scenes of interaction.

Wilhelm von Kobell painted many small pictures of the rural people around Munich either walking along a road to market or in conversation with bourgeois figures. *A Horseman and Two Peasant Girls* of 1829 is one of them. A bourgeois horseman seen against the church spires of Munich chats amiably with two attractive country girls in costume. Accompanied by his two dogs, he appears to address his inquiry to the prettier of the two peasants who

gestures in reaction to his question or declaration. The bourgeois is in control of his horse and capable of moving rapidly. The peasant girls are vulnerable and on foot in a vast landscape. The man can presumably make it to Munich easily. The women, although in sight of the great city, would be unable to walk there in a day. Their meeting on what appears to be a crossroad is a fleeting rapprochement between two classes who live, and will continue to live, in separate spheres.

Gustave Courbet chose to represent a similar subject in his *Young Ladies of the Village* of 1851. Two well-dressed bourgeois women (the painter's sisters) on a country stroll stop to chat with a young shepherdess who tends her cattle. There is a conspicuous difference in dress and posture between the small peasant girl and the young ladies of the title. Yet, unlike many other large-scale paintings by Courbet, it is difficult to read this work as criticism of class hierarchy. Rather, each of the classes seems to share both the countryside and the pleasures of this chance meeting. Indeed, it is no accident that the most shocking aspect of Courbet's painting when it was exhibited was not the subject, but the disproportionately small scale of the cattle with respect to the figures. In painting the *Young Ladies of the Village*, Courbet did not choose a subject as controversial as the *Peasants of Flagey Returning from the Fair* or *A Funeral at Ornans*, and there are even earlier popular

images of such cheerful class interaction. *The Visit to the Farmer* of 1842 is a lithograph made by Thierry-Frères representing a bourgeois family which has stopped to greet a farm family. By the position of the figures and their costume it conveys at once the conviviality and the basic differences between these two classes. One is reminded not only of François-André Vincent's picture *Agriculture* of 1798, but also of a late letter about the peasantry written by Camille Pissarro: "To think that one would have to live as peasants do in order to understand them properly. It seems to me that one must be carried away by one's subject in order to render it well, but is it necessary to be a peasant?... Let us first be artists and we shall then be capable of responding to everything, even a landscape, without being a peasant." Pissarro's letter and these pictures convey the message that peasant life is suitable for study but is not to be taken as a literal model for bourgeois life. In all these pictures, peasants are peasants, and bourgeois are bourgeois.

The nineteenth-century pictures which present the interaction of bourgeois and peasant with the greatest force and moral ambiguity are those painted in Brittany in the late 1880s by Emile Bernard. In *Breton Women in a Green Landscape* of 1888, Bernard created no harmony whatsoever between the standing or seated groups of costumed Breton women and the well-dressed bourgeois women sitting

Emile Bernard (1868-1941):
Breton Women in a Green Landscape, 1888.

together chatting in the background of the brilliantly acid green field. A pair of dogs is also segregated, in a sense balancing the pair of bourgeois women. Only at the far left of the picture is there a "mixed pair," two girls, one bourgeois and one peasant. As a whole, the painting abounds in discontinuities between peasant and bourgeois, adult and child, man and woman, and, finally, man and animal, and in celebrating these discontinuities Bernard is also suggesting that they are, in a certain way, analogous. Indeed, it was in the painting of the Pont-Aven group around Gauguin that the otherness rather than the accessibility of the peasant was best expressed, and Gauguin's own self-portrait in the country, *Bonjour Monsieur Gauguin*, makes it clear that his world and that of the female peasant are separate, and that the "Bonjour" offered by the peasant woman is more in politeness than in sincerity.

Paul Gauguin (1848-1903):
Bonjour Monsieur Gauguin, 1889.

The Peasant and the Market Economy

The nineteenth century was the great century of rural markets. In France the number of officially chartered markets grew steadily, both those connected with annual rural fairs and those held weekly or monthly. Markets became the focal point for small-scale exchange of produce on a local level, and as transportation became more extensive and more rapid the urban food market penetrated the countryside much more deeply than it had in the eighteenth century. A reader of Maxime Du Camp's description of the Paris market during the 1860s and of Zola's *Le Ventre de Paris* realizes that by the mid-century Parisian food and commodities came from throughout Europe and that small peasant markets collectively played a large role in the European economy. This growth of the rural market economy was a boon to the peasantry, many of whom found a ready market for cash sales and, as the century progressed, became less dependent on what Edmond About had called the ''vicious circle'' of the usurpation of their own food. More and more, peasants became petty capitalists.

The number of painted and printed representations of peasant markets is staggering. Indeed, one can safely say that the majority of pictures illustrating the modernization of the peasantry are market scenes. Some of them, like Wilkie's early *Pitlessie Fair*, depict peasant commerce within the context of a fair or festival which combines selling, dancing, performances, and usually religious observances of some kind. Many of them represent traditional fairs of long standing rather than more recently created peasant markets, and are best considered as part of the folkloric or ethnographic enterprise which was such an important feature of the peasant image. Other pictures like Toepffer's *Street Singer at an Italian Market*, show us an informal street market beneath Roman ruins and ask us to compare the grandeur of Rome with the petty capitalism of the present-day inhabitants. While Toepffer aimed at ethnographic accuracy in his depiction of the peasant costumes, he was not concerned with representing an important market in the context of a fair or dance.

Sir David Wilkie (1785-1841):
Pitlessie Fair, 1804.

Wolfgang Adam Toepffer (1766-1847):
Street Singer at an Italian Market.

Johann Fischbach (1797-1871):
Huckster at a Farmhouse, 1839.

Léon Lhermitte (1844-1925):
Apple Market at Landerneau, Finistère, 1878.

German painters were earlier than the French in their acceptance of peasant markets and commerce as a proper subject for art. Kobell's *Cattle Market before the Town of Constance* of 1820 is a superbly realized multifigural description of an enormous animal market with many kinds of bartering, trade, and payment. Johann Fischbach explored the phenomenon of an itinerant pedlar in his *Huckster at a Farmhouse* and, in choosing this subject, addressed himself to the various reactions of greed and selfishness of certain members of a rural household in the presence of a pedlar. He also makes it clear that, increasingly, peasant costumes were adorned with trade items and were not entirely the product of local handicrafts. Pedlars appear frequently as visitors and tricksters from the outside world in peasant fiction, and hence in illustrations. However, they were rarely painted in the nineteenth century.

There were so many paintings and prints of peasant markets in France during the second half of the nineteenth century that it is a subject itself for independent study. These works must be understood as having been made in the wake of a growing regional tourism in France, and the various guides from Joanne to Baedeker often contained information, both descriptive and factual, about particularly picturesque or unusual peasant markets. To visit a peasant market, to buy on the cheap, to enjoy the haggling over prices, were part of many country outings in the nineteenth century, and painted markets by Lhermitte and Pissarro tell us a great deal about rural commerce in the north of France during the last decades of that century. Generally, these two rather divergent artists chose to paint small-scale regular markets rather than fairs or markets connected with religious events. Lhermitte's *Apple Market* of 1878 was painted before any of Pissarro's market scenes and depicts a small regional market in a Norman village; there are no obviously bourgeois figures among the peasants. But at so specialized a market, dealing not only in apples but also in the increasing production of cider, quite a lot of money could change hands.

Wilhelm von Kobell (1766-1853):
*Cattle Market before the Town of Constance
on the Bodensee,* 1820. Pen and watercolour.

Camille Pissarro painted a series of peasant market scenes which, like those of Lhermitte, complete his cyclical investigation of peasant life. Both these artists, no matter how different in style and importance within the larger history of art, conceived of the peasant not as an isolated rural labourer engaged in growing his own food, but as an integral part of a larger economic order. Unlike Millet, Breton, and Bastien-Lepage, Pissarro and Lhermitte follow up the work of the fields to its natural outlet in the markets, and Pissarro's *Poultry Market at Pontoise* of 1882 represents a young female peasant with her wares surrounded by the intense human activity of the market. Whereas Pissarro's peasants are set amidst space and vegetation in his rural pictures they are pressed into an activated relief of overlapping human bodies in the market scenes. Their sales are conducted in a human arena alive with interest, an arena in which Pissarro explored the various tensions of class and sexual interaction. Surprisingly, he paid discreet homage to his predecessor Léon Lhermitte by borrowing a figure from that artist

Camille Pissarro (1830-1903):
Poultry Market at Pontoise, 1882.

Paul Sérusier (1864-1927):
The Cloth Woman, c. 1890.

Camille Pissarro (1830-1903):
The Market at Gisors, Rue Cappeville, 1894-1895. Etching.

for his etching *The Market at Gisors, Rue Cappeville* made in 1894–1895. This post-Impressionist market scene lacks the geniality of the earlier painting illustrated here, but can surely be read with the rest of Pissarro's peasant markets as a pictorial hymn to the interaction of city and country which would, for Pissarro, save the modern world from "embourgeoisement."

Finally, a Breton market scene painted about 1890 by Paul Sérusier. *The Cloth Woman* shows us how far the Pont-Aven group around Gauguin had come from the gentle petty capitalist genre painting of Pissarro and Lhermitte. For Sérusier, who centres his painting exactly on the frontal figure of the cloth woman, the market was the setting for a peasant rite and the dealer a priestess who offered goods to her suppliants. If these peasants are petty capitalists, their market economy operates by rules unknown to the city.

Oswaldo Tofani (1849-1915):
"Modern Agriculture."
Colour lithograph in *Supplément Illustré du Petit Journal*,
Paris, April 1897.

As early as 1860, the painter Daubigny executed an engraving showing a "machine à battre le blé" for the Paris journal *La Revue*, the mouthpiece of the newly formed Société du Progrès de l'Art Industriel. More than thirty years later, in 1897, a colour lithograph advertising the magazine *L'Agriculture Moderne* appeared in the *Supplément Illustré du Petit Journal*. Two figures, one a puzzled peasant wearing clogs, the other a clearly successful and well-dressed farmer, stand in front of a magnificent field of wheat. In the background is a mechanical thresher. The peasant asks his neighbour: "How did you get such fine wheat?"; and the neighbour replies: "Just do as I did, follow the advice of the penny magazine *Modern Agriculture*." Such pictures of peasant and machine, of the peasant confronting the modernization of his agrarian world, are rare, generally being found in publications like *La Revue* and *L'Agriculture Moderne*, which called for change and tried to persuade the newly literate peasantry of its advantages.

Not everyone approached the social and economic change of the rural world, particularly the mechanization of agriculture, with equal optimism. In the introduction to his book *Paysages et Paysans* (1898), illustrated by Léon Lhermitte, Marcel Charlot tells the reader that he was moved to write it not only to share with his compatriots his own patriotic and religious enthusiasm for peasants, but also because he felt that peasant life was threatened by the transition of fields into factories. In a similar illustrated lamentation, published a decade earlier, André Theuriet argued that only in poems and works of art would one continue to find the "charm and picturesqueness of rustic life."

In general, Theuriet's observation is vindicated in most of the paintings of peasant life made in the latter half of the nineteenth century. Pissarro's Norman peasants of the 1880s and 1890s are allowed none of the mechanized tools which were beginning to revolutionize Norman agriculture in those decades, and the same can be said for the peasants of Lhermitte, Bastien-

Georges Bellenger (1847-1918): *Farming in America.*
Ernest-Ange Duez (1843-1896): *La Jacquerie (The Peasant Revolt.)*
Illustrations in Emile Zola, *La Terre*, Flammarion, Paris, 1889.

Lepage, and Breton in France, of Waldmüller and Liebermann in Austria and Germany, and of a host of other painters of peasants throughout Europe. Even in literature one finds a similar tendency. Zola's peasants are woefully ignorant of the advances in chemical fertilization and mechanized ploughing or harvesting techniques. Only one wealthy and educated peasant in *La Terre* (1887) is familiar with the latest methods; his knowledge is fancifully illustrated in an engraving entitled *La Culture en Amérique* (Farming in America) which appeared in the 1889 Flammarion edition. Two peasants are chatting in the foreground, one eating his simple meal from a bowl. They are the past. In the background are machines harvesting the fields and telegraph poles carrying lines of communication between city and country. These are the symbols of the future. In keeping with Zola's aesthetic, however, the fate of this fictional modern peasant is not rosy. His farm collapses; he is ruined; and the backward village peasants interpret his downfall as a vindication of their traditional agricultural practices. In short, the undeniable agricultural progress which characterized a great deal of European farming in the later decades of the nineteenth century is virtually absent from the peasant image in literature, art, and even some social science. Almost in reaction to the changes which were disrupting the seasonal rhythms of labour and the pastoral quality of village life, image-makers clung desperately and effectively to the pre-modern peasant. Perhaps the most polemical statement of their view is to be found in the great French geographer Elisée Reclus's "open letter" to his "brother the peasant" published about 1894: "They will take your field and your crops away from you. You yourself will be taken and fastened to some iron machine, smoking and clanking, and all wrapped in coal smoke. You will have to rock your arms over a piston ten or twelve thousand times a day. This is what they will call agriculture." Reclus called upon peasants to band together against mechanization, urbanization, money, progress, tourism and so on; in short, against all the ills of the modern world.

Wilhelm Leibl (1844-1900):
The Village Politicians, 1876-1877.

The Peasant and Politics

In the same 1889 Flammarion edition of Zola's *La Terre*, there is an illustration entitled *La Jacquerie* which represents a peasant reading a book and imagining a crowd of his fellow peasants revolting with pitchforks in hand. The idea of the illustration is clear: that, through reading and intellectual improvement, peasants will realize their plight and rise up against their oppressors in the city. Although the implication that peasants are best left in their ignorance is to be found more in the illustrations than in Zola's text, it was a view widely held in the nineteenth century by those who feared any kind of lower class revolution against the values of industrial capitalism. As if in support of this view, many of the greatest social theorists on the left in the nineteenth century were contemptuous of the peasantry and placed their hopes for the future in the urban proletariat, much of which was composed, paradoxically, of men and women of peasant origin. Peasants themselves were strangely uninteresting as a political force during the nineteenth century, voting, when

they could vote, in various ways in various regions, for reasons which have more to do with the vicissitudes of local politics than with the larger issues of their day. The situation of the unpolitical or depoliticized peasant was sustained remarkably in the peasant image. There are few representations of peasant political uprising during the period, a fact reflecting both the wilful desire to segregate the peasantry from active participation in national decision-making, and the reality that there were few major peasant conflicts in a century devoted fervently on the left to the politics of the proletariat.

Perhaps the principal arena for peasant politics was the village pub, tavern, or café. Rare in the eighteenth century, these institutions gained ground steadily during the nineteenth and were, in themselves, responsible for what many later nineteenth-century students of rural life considered to be an alarming rise in peasant alcoholism and laziness. These problems were secondary, however, to the dramatic rise in political awareness on the part of the peasant due to the creation of these places for conversation and conviviality. Although many writers, especially Zola, show how insular and wrong-

headed this new tavern-based peasant politics
could be, politics it was, and, as if in support of
this idea, the painted representations of peasant
politics in the nineteenth century centred on the
tavern or café. Although David Wilkie painted a
scene of *Village Politicians* as early as 1806 and
set it in a rural Scottish pub, the two pictures
illustrated here come from the end of the
century. Leibl's *Village Politicians* painted in
1876–1877, represents a group of peasants not
at work in the fields, not at home with their
families, and certainly not at church, but in a
café. What is important is that they are reading
and talking rather than drinking and that Leibl
takes their politics seriously. He presents these
men struggling to understand the events of the
modern world. They are not ignorant peasants
driven by limited knowledge to violence, and
they are not the listless or decadent habitués of
the Paris cafés which figure so largely in the
work of Manet, Caillebotte, and Degas in the
late 1870s. The same idea of seriousness and
sobriety in the face of the modern world is
conveyed by Hodler in a fine picture, *Peasant
with a Glass of Schnapps*, of around 1890.
Working in the tradition of the peasant portrait
sanctioned by realism, Hodler shows a middle-
aged peasant having a glass of schnapps at a
table on which lies a copy of the *Feuille d'Avis
de Lausanne*. This incursion of an urban
newspaper into a rural milieu of slow time is the
true subject of the painting. The peasant, his
hands folded and his directionless gaze expressing his inward thoughts rather than his
openness, is turned from the paper which,
although facing him and within his reach, lies
unread on the table. The picture is ambivalent
about its subject: the peasant in touch with the
urban world, in this case Lausanne. Both these
paintings show us the growing modernity of
peasant life and, in the case of the Hodler
especially, raise questions about the nature of
the peasantry in such a context. Yet they are far
from being the most potent images of the
peasant within the political present, and there
are others which, while rare, convince us that
peasants did have a political life.

Ferdinand Hodler (1853-1918):
Peasant with a Glass of Schnapps, c. 1890.

François Grenier de Saint-Martin (1793-1867):
"Sauve qui peut": Peasants Stealing Wood, Surprised by a Rural Policeman, c. 1850. Print.

SAUVE QUI PEUT!

The idea of peasants revolting, even individually, against their situation is expressed more widely in literature than in art. A popular print like *Sauve qui peut*, one of several made at mid-century of peasants stealing wood, can best be read with the help of its literary counterparts as an image of a social class defying the authority of the government or of large property-owners. These pictures of defiance have never been studied as such, but they are joined, on occasion, by others of peasant solidarity like *At Gravelotte* by Albert Bettanier, of 1883. Here Bettanier represents a group of harvesters who are hiding a fugitive from the police. The print seems to side with the peasants rather than the police and it demonstrates the fear of police authority which was often noticed as a characteristic of peasant society in the second half of

Albert Bettanier:
"At Gravelotte": Harvesters Hiding a Fugitive from the Police, 1883. Print.

A. BETTANIER

A GRAVELOTTE, 1883

Jules Breton (1827-1906):
The Song of the Lark, 1884.

Franz von Defregger (1835-1921):
The Last Levy, 1874.

the nineteenth century. Louis La Garde, in his book *Nos Paysans: Etude de Physiologie Sociale* of 1902, wrote of the fear of any kind of authority, whether the police or the postman, under the chapter heading of "La Politique."

La Garde's next two chapters are entitled "Le Socialisme Agraire" and "Egoïsme" and, between them, they deal with what many political theorists thought to be the key problem of peasant politics, the possessive and individual spirit of the peasantry. For many nineteenth-century intellectuals, the peasant had no ability to organize, was jealous of everyone else, and was opposed at his base to any form of collective action. Marx likened peasant social organization to a "sack of potatoes" and there were many who agreed with him. Yet it would be wrong to dismiss the peasantry as a political force or to forget the many attempts, some successful, to organize rural workers into a collectivity . In 1874 Franz von Defregger painted an energetic and confrontational image of peasant organization in *The Last Levy*. In it, a group of alpine villagers have banded together, various weapons in hand, to march for a collective cause. Although aesthetically retrogressive in its profusion of picturesque visual details, Defregger's bold painting points the way to another which must be considered the most ambitious picture of peasants made in the last third of the nineteenth century, Pellizza da Volpedo's *The Fourth Estate*. Where Defregger was concerned with a collective action of costumed figures in a

charming rural setting, Pellizza avoids such details of costume and landscape scenery. His peasants are rural workers who are organized by him into a collectivity without weapons, a collectivity which advances with an almost hypnotic relentlessness towards the viewer. The figures are full-scale. Dressed not in "costume" but in their work clothes, they appeal to us, the bourgeois viewer, for justice as members not of the peasantry, but of the "fourth estate." Pellizza began his picture in November 1898 after nearly a decade of study and rural political action, and intended it to have the same sweeping political force as had Josef Mánes' Great Clock in Prague. Yet, while Mánes used the peasants of Czechoslovakia to embody the nationalist spirit with which he wished to see the Czech nation infused, Pellizza painted not on behalf of the village of Volpedo, not even of Italy, but of the modern world. His painting was an appeal to the world from the peasants.

In many ways, *The Fourth Estate* is the last great peasant picture and it must be read as the ultimate composition in a tradition of multi-figural modern history paintings begun by Robert and Schnetz, continued by Courbet, Breton, Millet, and Mánes, and ending with Pellizza. By Pellizza's time the peasant image had lost much of its potency, and his painting was little noticed when it was exhibited in Turin in 1901 and Rome in 1907. Indeed, the urban worker and the machines which he used proved to be more attractive subjects for twentieth-century painters of modern history, and the world of avant-garde art had finally moved from the fields of northern Europe with their rural workers to the cities which teemed with visual interest. It was in 1846 that Baudelaire appealed to the bourgeoisie and the cities they had created for the new and the modern in art, and it was the city which, after the triumph of Millet and Mánes, became the subject for the most viable of modern art. The peasant image was modernized especially in the second half of the nineteenth century, but the problems of the peasantry seemed small to a European world of unity and prosperity which had bypassed the peasant.

Giuseppe Pellizza da Volpedo (1868-1907):
The Fourth Estate, 1901.

EPILOGUE

PEASANTS AND FARMERS:
American Images of Rural Life

The word peasant has always been considered antithetical to the American way of life, rural or otherwise. Americans have generally perceived themselves in a utopian, positivist way, and their farmers are, and were in the nineteenth century, part of a modern capitalist system. American agriculture was mechanized well before that of Europe, and the popular image, literary or visual, of the single family American farm, filled with machines and almost bourgeois conveniences, was a standard one after the Civil War. Yet, if American agricultural machines and the popular prints illustrating their marvels flooded the trade fairs, international exhibitions, and popular journals of Europe during the second half of the nineteenth century, Americans had a converse, simultaneous, and insatiable desire for images of pre-modern European peasants. William Morris Hunt started a flood of French Realist peasant painting to America after his period of study with Millet, and, following his lead, Bostonians, notably John Quincy Shaw, established the most important collections of Millet and Barbizon school painting in the world. But the European peasant was sought more widely than in Boston, the most European of American cities. The paintings of Breton, Bastien-Lepage, and Lhermitte had an enormous market throughout America, and the works of these men and their lesser contemporaries can be found in the galleries and the reserves of art museums throughout the United States. Even in

Daniel Ridgway Knight (1845-1924):
Rural Courtship.

Minneapolis, a city at the centre of the American heartland, the entrepreneur James J. Hill, the first great collector of that region, built a private picture gallery in 1889 which contained several paintings by Millet, Israels, and Breton, including the *Song of the Lark*, now in the Art Institute of Chicago. The potency of this image of the peasant's hope and of his subjugation to the rhythms of the earth was felt as late as 1933 when visitors to the Chicago World's Fair voted it the most popular picture in America. Even today, its temporary removal from the galleries causes a flood of letters and telephone calls.

There is little doubt that the image of the peasant in the nineteenth century would have been a different one without the very considerable American market to stimulate its producers. For Americans, the peasant image was part of the larger picture of Europe itself and was therefore related to the development of the idea of America. Europe, as presented in exhibitions and private collections in nineteenth-century America, was more often than not a rural Europe, and Americans avoided images both of urban modernization in Europe and of her rich historical past. Perhaps the freedom, at least in dreams, that Americans felt from the grinding

fate of nature and the relentlessness of peasant life was celebrated in reverse through the peasant image as embodied by countless paintings in the drawing rooms and galleries of America's richest families. Perhaps too, images of these decent, God-fearing peasant families supported the idea that all Americans, great or small, had humble, often rural origins. Somehow it was easier to imagine one's forefathers as European peasants than as members of the urban proletariat.

Whatever the reasons, and they were certainly more complex than those mentioned here, Americans were devoted to the image of the peasant. One of these artists, the German-born Albert Bierstadt, who became the greatest nationalist landscape painter of America after the Civil War, started his career by painting the same Roman peasantry which so many other Europeans had pictured. Other American-born painters, like Eastman Johnson, who was trained in Düsseldorf, and Winslow Homer, who spent some time in France, turned their talents to the creation of American rural images not unlike those of peasants being produced by their European contemporaries. Eastman Johnson's *Corn Husking Bee*, as well as his series of

Eastman Johnson (1824-1906):
Corn Husking Bee, 1876.

Winslow Homer (1830-1910):
The Veteran in a New Field, 1865.

Eastman Johnson (1824-1906):
Winnowing Grain, 1873-1879.

Theodore Robinson (1852-1896):
The Cow Girl, 1888.

paintings of cranberry harvests, celebrate the collectivity of agricultural hand work in ways very similar to those of Breton, Lhermitte, Uhde, and others. Winslow Homer also conformed to these European patterns in a series of paintings of individual workers, like *The Veteran in a New Field* of 1865. Here Homer created an emblem of unmechanized labour not merely at the end of a season, but at the end of a war, and recalls to our minds the pictures of the *soldat-laboureur* painted by Vernet and Charlet and mentioned by Thiers in his *Salon de 1822*. For Homer, the American farmer was a peasant, and the analogy holds for other paintings like his superb *Girl with a Pitchfork* of 1867, which seems almost quoted from Millet or Breton. These paintings focused on the hard labour of the fields, a subject which became increasingly out of date as the relentless mechanization of the American farm continued, and only in these few canvases by Homer and Johnson does the American farm worker attain the emblematic stature of the European peasant.

Yet, if the American farmer proved unsuitable as a carrier for what were thought to be enduring values and ideas, the American painter could turn just as easily as his European counterparts to European peasants themselves. In fact, American artists played no inconsiderable role in the propagation of the European peasant image, and the greatest period of American collecting of European peasant paintings—the 1880s and the 1890s—coincided with the greatest period of American production of those images. Walter Gay painted the peasants of Brittany for the American market; Theodore Robinson constructed peasant images derived not only from Breton and Lhermitte, but from his friends Pissarro and Monet; Daniel Ridgway Knight turned out hundreds of French rural scenes; and Gari Melchers and others extended this range into Holland. All these painters conformed to the iconographical patterns which dominated the

Winslow Homer (1830-1910):
Girl with Pitchfork, 1867.

Gari Melchers (1860-1932):
The Sermon, 1886.

Walter Gay (1856-1937):
The Weaver, 1886.

European peasant image. For them, peasants were religious, hardworking, and family-oriented. Perhaps only the elements of nationalism and regionalism which were such an important substructure of the iconology of the European peasant image were lost on Americans in the nineteenth century. Indeed, only in the 1920s and 1930s, when American painting shirked its international role, did the American rural image play a part in the creation of an insular, defiant American nationalism. The peasant families of Millet, Liebermann, and Lhermitte are no match as icons for Grant Wood's masterpiece *American Gothic* of 1930. This farm couple with their hand tools and archaic clothing confront us with their decency and sobriety rather more than with their religious faith or their love. Grant Wood and his contemporary regionalists made images for a new nation in her first coming to grips with age, and their paintings and prints start another chapter in the larger history of the rural image.

Grant Wood (1892-1942):
American Gothic, 1930.

Bibliography and References

List of Illustrations

Index

References
to quotations in the text

p. 13 Muther, Vol. 2, p. 118.
p. 15 Léopold Robert quoted in Feuillet de Conches, p. 58.
p. 25 Roujon (1909), p. 16.
p. 27 Théophile Gautier quoted in Roujon, n.d., p. 51-52.
p. 27 Roscoe, p. 132.
p. 38 Fourcaud, p. 4.
p. 52 Weber, p. 12.
p. 59 About, p. 337.
p. 60 Lear, p. 103.
p. 67 Joanne, p. viii.
p. 75 *Salon de 1798*, p. 69.
p. 83 Paul Mantz quoted in Fourcaud, p. 23.
p. 90 Charlot, p. 7.
p. 99 Breton, p. 104.
p. 101 Breton, p. 111.
p. 108 Tuckerman, p. 72.
p. 119 Charlot, p. 7.
p. 124 Gower, p. 49-50.
p. 126 Pissarro, *Lettres à son fils Lucien*.
p. 135 Reclus, p. 55.

Bibliography
of works cited in the text

Edmond ABOUT, *Rome Contemporaine*, Paris, 1861.

William BRADFORD, *Sketches of the Country, Character, and Costume, in Portugal and Spain*, London, 1809.

Jules BRETON, *Un peintre paysan: souvenirs et impressions*, Paris, 1896.

Marcel CHARLOT, *Paysages et paysans*, Paris, 1898.

William H. DAWSON, *German Life in Town and Country*, New York and London, 1901.

George W. D. EVANS, *The Classic and Connoisseur in Italy and Sicily*, London, 1835.

F.S. FEUILLET DE CONCHES, *Léopold Robert: sa vie, ses œuvres et sa correspondance*, Paris, 1848.

L. de FOURCAUD, *Bastien-Lepage: sa vie et ses œuvres*, Paris n.d. (1885).

John GAGLIARDO, *From Pariah to Patriot: The Changing Image of the German Peasant, 1770-1840*, University of Kentucky, Lexington, 1969.

Lord Ronald GOWER, *Sir David Wilkie*, London, 1908.

Philip HAMERTON, *A Painter's Camp*, Boston, 1867.

Adolphe JOANNE, *Itinéraire général de la France: Bretagne*, Paris, 1867.

Louis de LA GARDE, *Nos paysans: étude de physiologie sociale*, Aix-en-Provence, 1902.

Edward LEAR, *Illustrated Excursions in Italy*, Vol. I, London, 1843.

Richard MUTHER, *The History of Modern Painting*, 4 volumes, London and New York, 1907.

Elisée RECLUS, *A mon frère le paysan*, La Brochure No 7, c. 1894.

Thomas ROSCOE, *The Tourist in Italy*, London, 1831.

Henry ROUJON, *Notice sur la vie et les travaux de M. Ernest Hébert*, Paris, 1909.

Henry ROUJON, *Les peintres illustres*, Vol. 37, P. Lafitte, Paris, n.d.

Alfred SENSIER, *La vie et l'œuvre de J.F. Millet*, Paris, 1881.

Walter SICKERT, "Modern Realism in Painting" in André Theuriet (editor), *Jules Bastien-Lepage and His Art*, London, 1892.

Hippolyte TAINE, *Voyage en Italie*, Paris, 1866.

André THEURIET, *La vie rustique: compositions et dessins de Léon Lhermitte*, Paris, 1888.

Henry T. TUCKERMAN, *The Italian Sketchbook*, London, 1848.

Eugen WEBER, *Peasants into Frenchmen: The Modernization of Rural France, 1870-1914*, Stanford University Press, Palo Alto, California, 1976.

Raymond WILLIAMS, *The Country and the City*, Oxford University Press, New York, 1973.

List of Illustrations

Index

SKIRA

BOOK DESIGN AND LAYOUT BY
LAURO VENTURI

PRINTED BY
IMPRIMERIES RÉUNIES S.A., LAUSANNE

BINDING BY
H.+J. SCHUMACHER AG, SCHMITTEN (FRIBOURG)